The
Pursuit
of
Acting

The Pursuit of Acting

Working Actors Share Their Experience and Advice

෬

Starra Andrews

PRAEGER

Westport, Connecticut
London

Library of Congress Cataloging-in-Publication Data

Andrews, Starra, 1961–
    The pursuit of acting : working actors share their experience and
advice / Starra Andrews.
        p. cm.
    Includes bibliographical references and index.
    ISBN 0–275–95692–X (alk. paper).—ISBN 0–275–96281–4 (pbk. :
alk. paper)
    1. Actors—United States—Biography. I. Title.
PN2285.A65 1998
792′.028′092273—dc21
    [B]   98–10919

British Library Cataloguing in Publication Data is available.

Library of Congress Catalog Card Number: 98–10919
ISBN: 0–275–95692–X
        0–275–96281–4 (pbk.)

First published in 1998

Praeger Publishers, 88 Post Road West, Westport, CT 06881
An imprint of Greenwood Publishing Group, Inc.

Printed in the United States of America

∞™

The paper used in this book complies with the
Permanent Paper Standard issued by the National
Information Standards Organization (Z39.48–1984).

10 9 8 7 6 5 4 3 2 1

Copyright Acknowledgment

The author and publisher gratefully acknowledge permission for the use of
biographical information and extracts provided by the actors. All essays are
printed with permission from the subject.

This book is dedicated to aspiring actors around the world and to their goals!

I also dedicate this book to my late grandmother Hazel Kellems, better known as "Gaga," for her energy, unconditional love, and constant support. She was also an actress for a brief time and a public speaker. Her most famous quote, which will live in our family forever, was, "Darling, you must project your voice!"

Contents

Preface

Years ago I was buying a new car and one of the salesmen struck up a conversation with me. He was a handsome gentleman who looked to be in his mid-fifties. He asked what I did for a living and I told him I was a secretary by day, but I was really an actress. All of a sudden his eyes lit up. "You're an actress," he said. Then he exclaimed, "I'm an actor too." He started telling me about the early days when he was acting in Hollywood. Throughout the 1950s and 1960s he did small film and television roles and various commercials. His boast was that he landed a supporting role opposite Rod Taylor in a western. When he spoke about his acting experiences he was a completely different person from the man I first met. I could tell he was starved to talk about acting with someone. I told him I was coming back the next day. He was pleased, and told me he would bring his 8x10 photos to show me.

The next day when I walked into the dealership, the gentleman made a beeline for me. He pulled his pictures out of an envelope and showed them to me with great eagerness. Most of them were of him in his earlier years. When he was putting the pictures away he told me about his last audition. When his agent called he got so excited, he put his old cowboy outfit on and raced over to the audition. When he walked in he was told the part was for a businessman. He didn't get the part and felt so foolish that he hadn't gone on an audition since.

I will never forget how he looked, his eyes full of despair. He shook his head, not understanding what had happened to him. I truly believe he thought he would have a successful career as an actor, and just got older, until he realized he had to work at something else. Eventually, that "something else" took over.

In February of 1995 I was sitting at my desk pondering how I had come to be a secretary for the past nine years. I suddenly thought about the gentleman I met and realized that I was starting down the same road he had traveled. Knowing that there are many student actors and other actors like me who could benefit from encouragement and guidance, I set out seeking advice from actors in the field. This book is the result. I hope it will inform and guide actors who are just starting out in their careers and refresh actors who are already working.

Acknowledgments

I want to express my thanks to a wonderful and talented friend, Dr. Maura Mitchell, for helping to create this book with her brilliant suggestion. I also need to express my gratitude to Mr. Rupert Holmes for giving me hope and courage many years ago. My husband, Lewis Hauser, has also been a support for me during the two years that I worked on this book, and I thank him for his ultimate patience and sense of humor on all those nights I ignored him and tapped away on the computer.

I especially need to thank Nina Pearlstein, who gave me the opportunity to have my book published and gave wonderful suggestions. I also thank my editor Elisabetta Linton, who guided me, as well as Susan Prusak and Rebecca Ardwin.

My family deserves my gratitude and they have been very supportive during the creation of this book. My mother Kaye Andrews, and my late grandmother Hazel Kellems helped me both financially and emotionally, and I thank them. My sisters Krista Andrews, Dr. Roxana Andrews, and Karen Andrews (who is actually my sister-in-law, but she's like another sister to me) have also supported me through some troubling times and I want them to know that I will never forget it, and I am very grateful.

I also thank Michael Arkush and Kate Benton, whose suggestions helped me in the early stages of the book proposal.

For putting me up in New York and completely going out of their way for me, I thank my friends Philip Mastrelli and Michael Pleshe.

The following people helped and supported me during this project and they deserve my thanks: Millie Kinsey, Fay Koliai, Brenda McDonald, Jana de Leon, Sue Reynolds, Tamara Mark, and all the "Pearl Girls"— Jill, Stacey, Marilee, Lisa, and Di. I need to give an extra thanks and I am very grateful to my friend Dr. Marilee Hanson, who helped me financially when I had to fly to New York and who believed in me. I also thank Karen Meyer, Lois Jones, and Ted Katzoff for referring actors to me for the book. Also, I thank Arthur Fuller for answering my bizarre technical computer questions and not laughing.

I respectfully thank the following acting teachers who took the time to read samples of my book for my publisher and give feedback. They are: Dr. Robert Cohen, Al Rossi, Fred Fate, Gary Carter, Jeff Sable, Janie Jones, Ted Walch, Curt Mortenson, Shirley Kaplan, and Maria Hepner.

On a personal note, I need to thank Julia Cameron (and her co-founder Mark Bryan) for creating the extremely helpful workbook *The Artist's Way*. When I started reading the chapters and going through the exercises, I was able to unblock creative fears that had been holding me back for *years*! The changes I made in my life helped me with the completion of this book. I recommend it highly to all actors.

Last, but not *at all* least, I wish to thank all the actors who let me interview them for this book. Not everyone I interviewed is in the finished product, but I thank everyone who participated and opened up their hearts and minds to help those actors who are pursuing their goal of acting at this moment. Without you this book wouldn't exist, and I thank all of you with a humble heart.

Introduction

"I just want to act, sing, and dance," I heard myself say to someone, and I know many other actors feel the same way. It takes devotion and courage to travel down the road of acting, since in addition to our pursuit we have to deal with paying the bills, rejection, and times of no work.

This book gives helpful advice on how to approach the everyday financial and emotional challenge of pursuing a career in acting. The actors interviewed are at different stages in their careers. Some are just starting out; others have frequented Broadway, film, and television. The suggestions given are yours for the taking. Of course, what works for someone else may not work for you. However, I hope you will find suggestions that will strike a chord with you, and help you creatively.

These actors candidly share their experiences and give words of advice at the end of each chapter. Some words of advice are simple and helpful, while others are encouraging, cautioning, inspiring, and spiritual. They also address dealing with rejection, slow periods when there's not much work, and issues of ethnicity.

The actors I have interviewed are at all different levels in their careers, from different backgrounds, and of various ages. In fact, you will find that some actors will not state their age in the introduction of a chapter because they feel it may limit them for playing different roles. Their experiences range from auditions, through various "day jobs," to close calls of the "casting couch."

This book is in two sections: actors interviewed in New York, and actors interviewed in Los Angeles. Many actors have trained and worked on both coasts, and many of them consider themselves bi-coastal. So, it's hard to put any actor in the category of New York or Los Angeles because there is a constant flow of actors between the two coasts.

Please take from this book whatever advice works for you, because all of the suggestions have been made with aspiring actors in mind, and are given with care and love for the craft of acting.

Part I

NEW YORK

Tamara Mark

Tamara has been working as a professional actress, dancer, and singer for seventeen years. She is originally from Portland, Oregon. She was cast in the first international tour of Michael Bennett's *A Chorus Line* and continued with the show when it came back to New York. Her Broadway credits also include Bob Fosse's *Dancin'*. She performed in *The Nutcracker* with the Chicago Ballet, and performed a season with the New York City Opera, and understudied singing roles in *The Merry Widow* and *Candide*. She was asked to lead auditions for *On Your Toes* directed by George Abbott. Once Mr. Abbott saw her dance and heard her sing, he cast her in the show, so she came back to Broadway. Her film debut was in *Fast Forward* directed by Sidney Poitier. She has studied with Peggy Feury and Stella Adler. Tamara has appeared in commercials and has done many voice-overs. Her television credits include appearances on *Cheers*, *L.A. Law*, *Twilight Zone*, *The Hitchhiker*, *Silk Stalkings*, *Sisters*, and a guest starring role on *Nash Bridges*.

I think I just came in knowing that this was going to be my destiny. My mother started me dancing when I was three years old, and I think that's highly unusual. I was also given piano lessons, and I was always taken to the symphony and to plays. My mom was a very pivotal person for developing creativity in me. It's what she always wanted to do but wasn't able to, growing up in the depression. I was also singled out since I was young to be in plays and dances. I was very determined and focused.

I started with ballet scholarships at eleven years old with the San Francisco Ballet and the Joffrey Ballet. That's what led me to acting. I would spend summers away from home in dance camps dancing fourteen hours a day, so the discipline started at a young age.

My friends talked me into auditioning for the open call in Portland, Oregon, for *A Chorus Line*. It was my very first theatrical audition even though I had been a dancer all my life. They hired me and I flew to New York City to be in the First International Company. I had never dreamed that I would be in a Broadway show, and I ended up being in one of the biggest Broadway musicals that ever hit the country. That's how I started acting, by being in a Broadway production, and I had never done any theatre in my life. The best teacher was being thrown into it. I already had the discipline, and I always knew I could act ever since I was a kid.

When I left the business for three days, I catered. I went down with the caterer in a cab to pick up the food and she looked at me and said "Tamara, what do you really do for a living?" She kindly told me I was meant to be in show business and she could tell. Working in the business is sometimes great, and sometimes hard, because there are leaner years than others. I think if actors have another interest, it's best to do something that will allow you to sustain your passion for acting. Do anything to achieve your dream, whatever job it is.

The highlight for me was working with legendary choreographers and directors. It was the best schooling I could possibly imagine. I'm like a sponge anyway, but when Bob Fosse, Michael Bennett, and George Abbott worked one-on-one with me, and gave me critiques about what they wanted to better in me, those were highlights. They were all mentors for me as an actress, dancer, and singer. Also, working with Sidney Poitier was one of the greatest experiences I ever had, because I always dreamed of being in the movies, and he gave me my dream. He actually called me personally on the phone when I booked the job. He left a message on my machine and said he would call me back. He did it because he remembered being an actor starting out, and he called the eight leads in the film and said, "You have been chosen to be in my movie." That is unheard of because it always comes through your agent or manager, so to have a man of his stature call me personally was the highlight of my career. That film was the fulfillment of all the things that I had dreamed of doing in one package with a great director and human being. Those type of experiences have helped me through slow times and helped me to persevere.

A low point for me has been getting close to being cast in different roles. I'm in a category where I'm up against the top people, and I did leave the business when things were about to hit for me, so the last four years have been a rebuilding of my career. The hardest thing has been the patience I've had to develop. Things happened so easily for me at the beginning that I didn't really understand, and I thought it would always be that way. There's a humility that has developed as well, which has made me feel more compassion for actors who are starting out. I pay the bills from being an actor, but I don't act at the expressive level that I know my talent is capable of, so I'm having to wait. I've been down to the end audition for television pilots and told I'm the favorite actress, and then nothing happens. It has been a test of my faith.

When auditioning, I try to get the script ahead of time and do my homework. Even if it's a small part in a movie, I read the entire script so that I know the essence of what the piece is about. I have to be ready to go in another direction if the person I'm reading with gives me something else, but I have to know what the character means to me. I've auditioned so much that it's rare when I get nervous. When the stakes are high, then I get a little nervous. If I talk to actors in the audition room, I go in and blow the audition, so I don't do that. I stay focused. I also stay off caffeine before an audition because it affects me.

After touring in *A Chorus Line* and moving to New York, my first audition was for Bob Fosse's *Dancin'*. I had a ballad to sing for the preliminary audition. The assistant told me I was coming back the next day to audition for Bob Fosse, but he told me to bring in an up-tempo song. Well, I had just arrived in New York, and I had no up-tempo song prepared. I called my vocal coach and he gave me a song to learn. Unfortunately, this song was really wordy and I had to learn it fast. That was the big mistake. Don't ever overextend yourself into a song or monologue you don't think you can handle learning the night before the audition. Even if you feel you know it cold the night before, I guarantee you, in the pressure situation of an audition, you will forget it. So, I got through the dance part of the audition fine. Then it came to the singing audition. I started my up-tempo song, got through the first line, and my mind went blank. So, I had to start again. I did that about four times. It was the worst nightmare of my life. So Mr. Fosse says to me "O.K., honey, don't worry, take a deep breath," and he came up on stage, held my hand, and looked me in the eye. He knew I was really young. He said "Let's do it again and don't worry about me, just do it." So I started the song and messed it up again. Finally I told him the whole story of trying to learn the song the night before. So he asked me if I had the ballad with me, and I didn't. So I learned another good lesson, to always have your back-up songs with you as well. He asked me if I knew "Here You Come Again," the Dolly Parton song, and I told him I did. So they started playing the song for me and I realized I actually didn't know it. Finally he let me sing part of "Yankee Doodle," and the whole time I could hear people in the wings saying "Why is he being so nice to her! She's not prepared!" So I'm hearing this as well. He let me look at the lyrics of my song again, then try it, and again I messed it up. By this time, I felt two inches high. He told me to go backstage and write the lyrics down on a piece of paper and when everybody else had sung, I could come back out and sing. I could hear people saying "Oh, brother! I can't believe he's being so nice." He had narrowed it down to twelve dancers and he only needed two. This was after an initial cattle call of about eight hundred. So I really didn't think I would get the job, but I figured he liked me, so maybe the next one I would have a chance. He lined us all up on stage and it felt like the end of the audition, so the dance captain said, "What about Tamara's song?" He said, "That's right, Tamara hasn't sung again." At this point I could *feel* people rolling their eyes! So I went out on stage with the piece of paper and I still messed up the lyrics, but I got through the entire song. Everyone applauded me, people in the audience, the wings, everyone, because they couldn't believe I got through it. Then he lined us all up on stage again, came up to me, took me by the hand, and said, "Congratulations, you got the job." I ended up having a lot of the singing parts in the show as well as the dancing. I think he liked my vulnerability, because people told me he could be really cruel to people who were not together, but he knew the level of my talents and that is why he hired me. I was also a little scared of him because of his legendary stature and presence.

When you're looking for an agent, make a video of your work because they really do want tape. If you're in a play, make sure it's taped. Also, get yourself in commercials. Pick a small number of agents you will mail your pictures to. I got a manger, who helped me get an agent.

I booked jobs with my manager, because casting directors knew my manager. Get yourself in a theatre company or in workshops or seminars where they hold an agent showcase night. I think those work.

The way I handle rejection is by being a firm believer that when it's my job, it's my job. My life has been an example of that. Things just happened to me, but I had also worked very hard since I was a little girl. I don't deal with it as rejection anymore, because I feel that if it's my destiny, the right jobs are always going to come my way. It has really helped me surrender. It's easy to get devastated, and I've seen people turn to drugs and alcohol. So I just remember that the producer may know someone, or they may go for another look, so it's not even about talent sometimes. Actors shouldn't beat themselves up. I booked a major Broadway show and I had the worst audition anyone could ever imagine happening.

What keeps me going is the fact that I had the opportunity of leaving and coming back to the business. I know that I'm not coming back for the fame, the glory, or the money (all the things that I hear people say they want). I'm here for the pure joy and love of what I do.

WORDS OF ADVICE

- First and foremost, you have to be involved in acting not just for the rewards of glory or fame. You have to do it because it's the reason you get up in the morning.
- Have patience and don't give up, because it happens for everybody differently and at different ages. I firmly believe there's room for everybody.
- Start out with a small agency that has a lot of clout.
- Even if you're waiting tables or working a straight job, tell people you're an actor. Don't be embarrassed by your temporary employment.
- Do something that keeps you in touch with the creative child in you. It's key to keep the creativity flowing.

Danny Koch

Danny is thirty-seven years old, originally from New York, and has been pursuing acting for seventeen years. His theatre credits include *Stand by Your Beds Boys*, *Lost Angels*, *Citizen Bellow*, and *Marat/Sade*. Danny's film and television credits include *George Schlatter's Comedy Club* (NBC), *Zamboni* (AFI), *My Womb and Welcome to It*, and *Feldner's Dream* (USC). He has also done many commercials domestically and internationally. Danny has performed stand-up comedy in Los Angeles at the Comedy Store, Laugh Factory, and L.A. Connection. In New York he appeared at Caroline's, Improvisation, and Comedy Cellar.

Growing up in New York, and having a very New York family—my grandmother was very into the arts—we went to the theatre a lot. When we would see a Broadway show, I always got a special jittery feeling when the audience would applaud at curtain call. That feeling always translated into one thought: "Gosh, I could do that. I would love to do that." I still have that same feeling when I go to the theatre today as an audience member. It's a very sacred type of feeling that I don't experience anywhere else.

I have been making a living consistently for eight years from my commercials. I've been doing commercials for fourteen years at an average of four to fifteen a year. I always wanted to make a living from acting, and I wanted to have some identity as an actor, which I have, because people sometimes recognize me. I've also gotten to travel. I've been to Italy three times to shoot commercials, staying in beautiful hotels each time. They were Italian commercials for Italian companies. Through the commercials, I have put together a nice little career for myself. The problem, in my specific case, is that because of the success I have had with commercials, I haven't felt as much pressure to beef up the other sides of my career as much as I should have. I still take classes from time to time, but I don't push myself as much, because I have this income that magically arrives at the mailbox. I already have my pension from SAG when I retire, and health benefits.

When I first started working, I worked at the Comedy Store in Los Angeles. When comedians start out there, they make you work the door. That's so you get to know the comics, you get to know the club, and every now and then, you get to perform. One night I was working the door and Richard Pryor came in. I was also the emcee that night, so I went on stage after his performance was done and said "Ladies and gentlemen, Richard Pryor." Everyone applauded him. I was announcing the next act, and said "Our next act" and someone from offstage yelled "Isn't ready." There I was on stage, so I launched into my routine for five minutes and did really well. Following Richard Pryor and getting laughs was an accomplishment. Sometimes I think not being prepared works just as well.

A definite low point was when I got a lead role in an equity-waiver play in Los Angeles, in a very dysfunctional production. I was actually a replacement because someone left the show and they had been rehearsing for two weeks, so I was at a disadvantage to start. They already knew their lines and I walked in and saw that things weren't quite right, and within ten days of getting this great role, that I was very excited about, I got fired. At the time, it was incredibly painful. I've thought of that experience, and I thought I sucked. I started to second guess myself, and doubt. In this business, there is enough second guessing, doubt, and fear, without someone validating it for me by firing me. It took me a little while to get back on the horse after that experience. In retrospect, there was really nothing I could do, it was a no-win situation.

I think each audition is different. Each script is different. I'm very good with comedy, so if someone hands me a script, I don't have to figure out what's funny. It's funny, or it's not funny, and I know how to do it. If I get a dramatic piece, I seem to put a lot more emphasis on it. I try to change the nervousness into excitement. A casting director once told me, "Don't think of yourself as being nervous, think of yourself as being excited." It's a cool little trick, because it's cool to be excited.

The first commercial I auditioned for was two other guys and me sitting at a dinner table singing "Happy Birthday." I was one of two guys on the outside singing to the guy in the middle. When we got to the line "Happy birthday dear," I realized I hadn't gotten the actor's name. So, instead of singing nothing, I sang "Happy birthday, dear dickface, happy birthday to you." The casting director laughed, and the other actor walked outside and said "Why did you call me dickface?" I said, "I'm sorry, I just didn't know your name," and three days later, I got my first commercial.

Right now, I just have a commercial agent. In the past I have done many things to try to score good agents. At one point, I had a shirt that I always wore to auditions if I were playing a gas station attendant. It was one of those blue shirts with the name patch on it. I would put my picture and resumes in Federal Express envelopes, that I got from the Federal Express office, and I typed all the labels to make it look like it was coming Federal Express. I walked around to the agents and handed them to the receptionist myself. I found that that was more interesting than just sending pictures and resumes, because I've been to agent's offices and seen that a lot of times the envelopes aren't even opened. I have another friend who used to send lottery tickets attached to her headshot, and she wrote on a note, "I am a winner, and hopefully by scratching this off you'll be a winner too. Please call me because I would love to meet you." I find that there's always another angle. You can call until your fingers turn blue, but trying to get a good agent is a major stumbling block. Get into a great show and tell them, "Come see me, I'm brilliant."

I've been doing this now for many years, and at times I think I have a handle on it and at times I just go "Ouch!" I don't think actors handle rejection, they manage rejection. When there are jobs out there that you auditioned for, you know you're right for the role, you gave a good reading, and you don't get it, it's still painful. I think that if it's not painful, then it probably doesn't mean as much as it should mean. I think it's O.K. for actors to feel the pain. Let it sink in and move on.

WORDS OF ADVICE

- Have a firm foundation. Play as many roles as you can, in as many types of theatre as possible.
- Involve yourself with as many different people, theatre companies, and student films as you can.
- Get as much exposure as you can. You're going to learn something from every experience you have, negative or positive.

Garry Pastore

Garry is in his early thirties and is originally from New York City. He has been pursuing acting professionally for sixteen years. He studied with acting teachers in New York, and his theatre credits include *Love Lost* at the Westbank Theatre, *Crazy Horse* at the Players Loft, *Mulberry Street* at the Actors Playhouse, and *Loose Ends* at the Circle in the Square. His feature film credits include *Men Lie*, *Copland*, *The Devil's Own*, *Carlito's Way*, *A Bronx Tale*, *GoodFellas*, *Do the Right Thing*, *Cocktail*, and *Prizzi's Honor*. In television, Garry has been seen in *Path to Paradise*, *Mistrial*, *Swift Justice*, *The Wright Verdicts*, *Loving*, *Ryan's Hope*, and *The Cosby Show*.

I was always a child who would try to put on a show for family and friends. I love the act of entertaining and making people happy. In high school, one of my English teachers was also a drama teacher. He grabbed me after class one day and said, "You're very entertaining and you sing well! Why don't you be in one of my productions?" He had come to the battle of the bands and heard me sing. He said he was going to direct *West Side Story*, and asked if I would audition for it. I told him I wouldn't cut my hair, and he told me I would have to. Well, he kept pressuring me enough that I finally did it. I wound up getting the part, cut my hair, and got bitten by the bug.

I got a job at a restaurant called Columbus, which is now out of business, but it was like a Spago. It was very popular with people in the entertainment business. The restaurant business is probably the best, because you can work nights, and you can get someone to cover for you if you get a job. You have to make a living in this business, because if you're not paying your bills, you're not going to be a good actor. You have to have a clear head when you're out there auditioning.

I don't think I can say I've had a highlight yet. A highlight would be me getting a lead role in a film. I co-starred in a film called *Men Lie* two years ago, and I was really excited. We won two film festivals in Texas and Florida, but the film never went anywhere. It's still sitting in the can. Now I try not to get too excited, because if something doesn't happen, I don't want to get jaded. I would like to start making a living as an actor. I would like to be self-supporting.

Go into an audition and be that person. If you have to be Rocko the armbreaker, leave the house and be Rocko the armbreaker. From the time you leave the house, until you get into the audition room, until you sit with the casting director, stay focused on the character. Try not to get distracted by traffic and the elements.

Here's an example of being in the right place at the right time. I went to a casting director seminar and did a reading for a casting director from a popular soap. He told me, "You're wonderful, you're great." and said "You'll be hearing from me." Sure enough, I never heard from him. Two years passed, I moved to Manhattan and was working in a restaurant. I was a doorman/assistant manager. It was two o'clock in the morning, I had locked the doors, and a jeep pulled up. A man hopped out and knocked on the door. I said "Can I help you?" He said "We want to come in for a drink," and I told him the restaurant was closed. I told him the bar across the street was open and to go over there, we were closed. He said "No, we want to drink here." When I still said no, he told me that he worked at ABC Studios, so I asked him what he did there. He told me he was a casting director for a particular soap. I said "Wait a minute. I auditioned for you two years ago, you told me how great I was, and then you didn't let me read like you said you were going to. Now, why should I let you in?" He said "You actors are all alike. What is this, blackmail?" I said "Yeah, I guess it is, isn't it. You want to come in for a drink, and I want to get on your show. I'll make you a deal. I'll let you in for a drink if you let me read." He said "All right. Give me a call tomorrow." So I let him and his date in. Then I went in and read, got a part on the show, and got in the union. I was in a position where I held the trump card for a change.

What keeps me going is that there's no other business like it in the world. It's a rush of adrenaline every time I'm on a set. There's also frustration on a set when you're waiting around, but when you feel that way, remember where you came from. Remember what it was like not to work. It's a respect. Respect the actor who is doing the same thing that you did.

WORDS OF ADVICE

- Every person that I've met in the business, I will run into once again. Once you build up that rapport, and have respect with those people, chances are you are going to be able to work with them again.
- If you start to lose respect as an actor, or act like a jerk, people are going to find out and they're not going to work with you.
- I met people who have been in the business for a year, and they're upset because they haven't worked yet. You can't put a time limit on it. It really has to come from within.
- You have to be frugal. Try to save money.
- Get up every day, shrug off the negativity, suck in the positive, and appreciate the fact that you're doing something that you want to do.

Emma Palzere

Emma is thirty-four and is originally from Newington, Connecticut. She has been pursuing acting professionally for twelve years. She holds a B.F.A. from Emerson College in Boston, and has been seen Off-Broadway in *Waiting Women*, *Nighthawks*, *Born in the R.S.A*, *Montage*, and *The Rimers of Eldritch*, among others. Emma can also be spotted in various films, soaps, and commercials, and is a company member of Murder by Invitation, and Carousel Theatre Company of New York City. Her company, Be Well Productions, currently tours throughout the Northeast with three productions: *The Belle of Amherst*, *I.C.U.—Improv Comedy Unit*, and *Live from the Milky Way . . . It's Gilda Radner!*, which recently won the Warner Center for the Arts One Act Play Contest (Torrington, CT) and is headed for a full production Off-Broadway. In 1990, Emma banded together with other female solo theatre artists to create Womenkind, an annual festival of one-woman shows celebrating women's history month.

From the time I could talk, I wanted to be a ballet dancer. I studied ballet throughout my childhood, but I clearly didn't have the physical stamina to make it professionally. I was one of the best dancers at my school, but I wasn't the right body type. Whenever we did ballets, the whole class would get cast in various roles, and while everyone else would be gingerbread people, I would be the one peppermint stick. So I started at that age learning to be a character actor, because I had my own style. I finished high school a semester early, and I wanted to go into the theatre but had no real training. My guidance counselor and parents suggested I do an internship at one of the theatres in Connecticut. I opened the Yellow Pages, wrote to all the theatres, got several interviews, and ended up doing an internship in the props department at the Hartford Stage Company. I worked there on and off for the next three years behind the scenes, and it was one of the most invaluable experiences I ever had. That internship got me other internships, where I was then able to act or understudy. Not knowing how professional theatre worked, I learned so much. The first day I walked in, I thought, "This is where I belong." What I learned didn't go to waste, because I use all that knowledge today.

I worked for a year in regional theatre. I was the only female intern in this theatre, with a nice stipend, which in Indianapolis was a living wage. I came back to New York with my Equity card, and no work. I had been really spoiled. There was nothing to do but get up at 7:00 A.M. and stand on audition lines. It was horrible. It was not a creative experience, and it was not fulfilling in any way. However, I got up and I did it. If actors don't line up by 8:00 A.M., they'll never get seen before the end of the day, because there are so many actors. You get two minutes maximum, and you're auditioning for the assistant to the casting director of a show that already has stars in it. After a couple months of that, I thought, "This isn't why I came to New York." I recognized that I needed to be a fulfilled person, and to help my career, so I started producing tours of one-woman shows. At that time, I thought it would be a creative project for a few months that wouldn't interfere with my auditioning. I thought of it as something to focus on to make me feel better about myself. Seven years later, it's a job that I get paid for, and it makes me an artist.

What I do for part of my income is produce work that I tour in. You have to be willing to go outside of New York. People will also ask me how much I really make from this, and even if I make $150 working for an hour, it's as much as I would make spending eight hours in an office somewhere, and it makes me an actor. I now produce a festival of one-woman shows, that's a networking and support system for a lot of ac-

tors who have discovered this kind of work to continue acting. I'm
working as a production manager for a nonprofit touring company
called Plays for Living, and I also have the opportunity to perform with
them. It's flexible enough that I can still do my own work, and audition, and it uses all the skills I've developed over the years. Also, for
the first time in my life I have a weekly salary and benefits.

A highlight for me was extra work I did on a movie called *Night
Falls on Manhattan* directed by Sidney Lumet. I was in a group of special extras, and we were assistants to the District Attorney in the same
group with Andy Garcia's character. So we had to be in the same
scenes with him in those situations. Watching Sidney Lumet work was
an amazing experience. He was so organized, loved what he was doing,
and knew what he was doing. When we went back for the second day,
they called us into a room and he pointed at me and said, "What's your
name?" I told him, and he said, "O.K., the first shot of the day is going
to be of you." It was so exciting that that was the way the day started
and to be treated so well. They called us by our names, not by num-
bers.

The one-woman show I wrote, *Live from the Milky Way . . . It's
Gilda Radner!* has also been a highlight for me. The show is about
Gilda from the afterlife, and she doesn't know if she's still funny because she's died of cancer. I use her characters, and a few new characters. What makes the difference between an actor and an artist, is that
after getting suggestions from people, I realized I had reasons for
choosing every word I chose, what to put in the story, what not to put in
the story, what to highlight in a comedic way, and what to highlight in a
serious way. Those were all conscious choices. As an actor in the
business, you don't always get control over what you're doing, or you
don't have the ability to explore it. You can lose sight of being an artist.

A couple of producers saw my performance of *Live from the Milky
Way . . . It's Gilda Radner!* without my pursuing them aggressively. I
only sent them a postcard. They came to the show, and walked out in
the middle, very obviously. However, I knew I had to make a follow-up
call to them. So I dutifully made my phone call, and after I told the
secretary who was calling, the producer immediately snapped up the
phone. All he said was "Hi, Emma. Let me tell you what I didn't like
about your show." This man talked for an hour nonstop. All I could do
was say, "Uh, huh." It was not constructive criticism, and I was prepared to tell him I was interested in feedback because the play was still

in development, but I couldn't even get that out. He just went on telling me what he didn't like about what I had invested a year and a half of my life in. So it's those kind of moments that can chip away at one's self-confidence.

I think preparing for auditions changes and evolves all the time. For me, a lot of it lies in the technical things, like having my photo and clothes ready the night before so that I'm not distracted. It sounds like external stuff, but the performance part of it I trust; it's all the outward things that can distract me. When you're at cattle-call auditions, the chatter from actors in line can be distracting, and it's usually trivial and annoying. I usually bring something to read or wear headphones. It's a signal to other people that I want to block out the talking. I also have three things ready that I want them to know about me, and three things I want to find out about them. So, if there is an opportunity for conversation, I have a focus of what I want to say, and I know it's appropriate.

Rejection is not personal rejection. I think it's just separating yourself from the you that's the product your selling, and you, the human being. They are two different things. I've had enough experiences not getting a job, and then getting a call a year later because they remembered me. Just because you don't get a job doesn't mean there's no possibility of a working relationship with the people you've auditioned for. Remember that there are other possibilities that may come out of an audition other than yes or no.

What keeps me going is I feel I have a mission. I feel I have things to do that I haven't done yet. When I started to produce my own work, I got back in touch with the question of why did I become an actress, and what do I want the audience to get out of it? I work with using a purpose, and having a greater purpose for my work that's outside of me. For me that's to be a channel for healing. Not all acting work I do will be that, but it gives me a purpose and a vision that's beyond making x amount of dollars, or having an agent.

WORDS OF ADVICE

- At the beginning, say yes to everything you can do, even things like ushering for free, and jump right in.
- See as much performance as you can and do as much performance as you can. That's the only way to learn.

5

Veronica James

Veronica has been actively pursuing acting for five years. She is originally from New Jersey but also grew up in Europe. She received a B.A. in Communications and Performing Arts from William Paterson College and has trained with British and American acting teachers. Her Off-Broadway credits include *The Good Child, Vacancy, High Risk Giving, Under the Same Roof, Possessed/Dracula Musical, The Glass Menagerie*, and many classical roles. Her film credits include short independents *Seefood* produced by Sigourney Weaver, *An Urban Legend*, appearances on *One Life To Live, Central Park West, Under the Hammer* (BBC), a sitcom for NYU, and Woody Allen's *Bullets Over Broadway*. She has also appeared as an alien on the Sci-Fi Channel. Veronica played a principal role in the feature film *Five Dead on the Crimson Canvas*, which was screened in New York and won an award at the Fanta Festival in Rome.

I grew up with the arts, and I started in dance when I was six years old. I've always been drawn to self expression and performance. I can't live within only a mundane existence. I feel incomplete without self-expression. I chose to become an actor because I wanted a profession in which the essence of my being would be utilized creatively, as opposed to just a skill that I could do detached from myself. I wanted the essence of me to be the product.

I've done freelance work, trade show work, and industrial promotions. I also do fragrance modeling, temporary office jobs, various part-time jobs, and I try to keep everything as flexible as I can. I try to be workable, and very professional about everything that I do, never forgetting that I'm an actor.

Find a job that is not so all-encompassing that it takes away from your creative focus. Let the people know straightaway that you're an actor, and very often you'll be in a supportive environment and have flexibility for auditions. I think it's really important that your environment is supportive and not stressful. I can't recommend a specific job, because it varies from actor to actor. Some people like to type and some people like to wait tables. It depends.

A highlight for me was having a starring role in the feature length film *Five Dead on the Crimson Canvas*. It's an independent artistic film and I'm very proud of my work in it. The biggest career highlight for the process of being an actor is the process of self-discovery and growth. My own personal evolution as an artist. I can see it unfold, and it's very exciting.

A low point was a few years ago. Artistically, I was very unfocused and I didn't have myself together in terms of my marketing. My audition material was not the best suited for me, I wasn't doing well in auditions, I was not in a good acting class, and my self-image was not clear. This was a frustrating time for me, because I felt professionally I was really going nowhere, and I didn't know what to do about it. So I took some time off from the business to do other things that weren't acting related, and I traveled. I knew I would get back into the business, though, and when I did, I started working with a marketing coach. She formed me, taught me how to market myself, how to think of myself as being successful, and that changed my life. I found that people I had submitted pictures to, who didn't call me, were now calling me after submitting my new pictures, and didn't realize that I had submitted previously. So I'm having much more success now.

To prepare for an audition I do my homework first and foremost. If it's a play, and it's available, I read the play and try to get to know as much about the character as I can. I think very visually, and I try to see the character in my imagination. To clarify the image, I sometimes will sketch the character to make the image more concrete. I also make a point, in a practical sense, to plan and check carefully the entire wardrobe I'm going to wear to the audition to create the illusion of the character.

When I went to the audition for *Five Dead on the Crimson Canvas*, I was not given any sides, I was just given a half page character description and biography. It was so well written that I was able to get an immediate picture of the character. I started working and preparing myself from my imagination. I even dressed myself and put on make up so it would represent what I saw. When I got to the audition I had all of my techniques going that I work with, and after the reading was over, the director looked at me and said, "You read that exactly as I envisioned it." That was wonderful to hear, because many times you're not told whether they liked it or didn't like it. That was a very good situation. The point is, I went with my instincts. I went with my gut feeling, and I got it, because I believed so much in what I felt. Also, I was fortunate to have a very well-written script. Now I feel that whatever they throw at me I can do. Whatever they throw at me I can throw back.

Don't make the idea of getting an agent a means to an end, because it isn't. It's important to go to seminars, meet with agents, listen to what they say, and keep in touch with them. Invite them to your showcases, screenings, and let them know when you're performing. Don't just send a postcard to send a postcard; stay in touch with them when you have something to say, otherwise, the postcards just clutter up their desks. Let them know that you're consistent, because eventually the right agent will come to you. Also, agents like it when you do most of your own work. Once you get an agent you can't just sit back and say "I don't have to work anymore." That's not true, you still have to get most of your work on your own.

I don't take rejection personally. Remember that there are always other projects. Besides the trade papers, always read bulletin boards at film schools, and at the Equity and SAG offices. Don't take it personally if you don't get a job; perhaps that job wasn't the right thing for you. The right job will come to you. Just go on to the next audition.

Being an actor professionally has an enormous amount of demands. It takes an enormous amount of tenacity, stamina, and a strong will, all of which I have. Part of what keeps me going is that I'm a very hardworking person and I enjoy the challenge of finding the next part, molding myself into a character, and stretching my imagination. In researching different parts, I have been able to read everything from the history of Western America to Russian poetry. It's a wonderful, all-around educational experience. I am sometimes asked "Is it glamorous being an actor?" I say, "I go to the library and the post office a lot because I read and send lots of mail!" However, there are little magical moments in the process of the acting itself that I live for. It gives me great joy and self-pride when I know I've done the best that I possibly can. When those moments happen, your training is in place, and you know you're really prepared, it makes everything else worthwhile. In order to get to those points you have to have a strong will, pride, a lot of energy, and you have to keep going. It's the people who have all that, that will stay in it. Many people know how to act, but don't know how to be actors!

WORDS OF ADVICE

- Know your marketing, and know yourself as an individual.
- Have a good sense of professionalism.
- Have a good sense of a balance between art and business.
- Develop strong instincts and learn to trust your instincts.
- Keep your health good and focus on nutrition and exercise. Get good rest, and keep yourself physically as optimum as you can.
- Study and train with the teachers you feel are right for you.
- Talk to lots of people in the business and ask questions.
- As a professional actor, you are the CEO of your corporation. Everyone you go to for your business, whether it's a photographer, an acting teacher, resume specialist, or a marketing coach, is being hired and paid by you to help you do the best job you can.
- At auditions, be as professional as possible and listen to all your directions. Listen to everything that's said, and ask questions if you're not sure. Also, ask if you can ask a question. Remember, it's your time as a performer. It's your audition, just have fun with it.
- Carry a notebook everywhere. Keep a journal and reflect on your evolvement.
- Have a balance of life outside of acting. Solidify your personal life as much as possible. You don't have to be "on" all the time.

6

Calvin Remsberg

Calvin is forty-six, originally from Virginia, and has been pursuing acting for twenty-five years. He graduated from William and Mary and continued with graduate work at George Mason University. He studied voice with Dr. Wilbert King, Anne Rowe, and Frederick Wilkerson. Calvin is best remembered as The Beadle in the national tour and award-winning television production of *Sweeney Todd* with Angela Lansbury. He also starred in the national tour of *Cats*, and portrayed Firmin, the crotchety opera-house manager opposite Michael Crawford, Robert Guillaume, and Davis Gaines in the record-breaking Los Angeles engagement of *The Phantom of the Opera*. He also played the Padre in Long Beach Civic Light Opera's *Man of La Mancha*. He has appeared in numerous films and television shows, including *Pretty Woman*, *The Water Engine*, *Cheers*, *Nurses*, *The Young and the Restless*, *General Hospital*, and *Twilight of the Golds*. Calvin is also the musical theatre director of the California State Summer School of the Arts, maintains an active private studio in voice and is currently preparing a book entitled *Voice for the Theatre*.

In 1963 I had a wonderful science teacher named Mrs. Torpy. We were talking one day and I told her I didn't know what to get my parents for Christmas. She asked me if they ever attended the theatre, because there was a new musical coming to the National Theatre in Washington right around Christmas. She said if I brought her the money, she could get me tickets. So I told my parents I needed money, but I didn't tell them what it was for, and I got tickets. We had three seats to see *Hello, Dolly!* before it went to Broadway. It was on a try-out tour. The night we went, Gower Champion came out in front of the curtain and said "Ladies and gentlemen, we are putting in a new first act finale tonight, but the sets and costumes aren't ready. We're going to do it anyway, but since there are no sets and costumes, we're going to do the old finale first, then back up and do the new one." I saw the very first public performance of "Before the Parade Passes By." Well, I was thirteen years old, and when Carol Channing came down those steps in that red dress I was hooked. That was it! I knew that's what I had to do (not in a red dress, mind you). A sideline to this is that when I was performing in *Cats* at the same theatre in Washington, Mrs. Torpy came to see me.

To help out financially I sang in a church choir and a synagogue. So I was a Jew on Fridays and an Episcopalian on the weekends. To really make ends meet, though, I started substitute-teaching in English, theatre, and music. Substitute-teaching is a very good job; while it doesn't pay a lot of money, you can say no and not jeopardize your job. Avoid any job that uses your voice strenuously. For two years I taught music, and during that time I had several opera auditions. At one audition the conductor said "You teach, don't you?" I said "Yes," and he said "Quit." I flew home from that opera audition and quit. I was using my voice too much because the students I taught were young, their voices were loud and I'd have to shout them down to keep them quiet. So I taught drama where the kids had to talk, but I didn't.

The highlight for me without a doubt was performing in *Sweeney Todd*. As I was growing up, I listened to all of the Stephen Sondheim and Hal Prince musicals and I loved their work. My dream one day was to be in one of their shows. One night my vocal coach, who was also an assistant conductor with the Washington Opera, walked into one of our rehearsals and said, "I've just seen *Sweeney Todd* and there's a role in it for you." Then he sat down at the piano, played music from the show, and said, "Listen to this." I thought it was wonderful, but I was living in Washington, D.C., and I was a school teacher. I didn't know how I would be able to do it. It's amazing how the pieces of the puzzle fit together. My friend Glenn Close was in New York performing in *Barnum* and happened to know Len Cariou, who was playing Sweeney Todd on Broadway. One night I came into town and we all went out to dinner. At the close of the evening, Len turned to me and said, "You know, you'd be perfect for The Beadle in *Sweeney Todd*. Do you sing at all?" I said "Yes." So they arranged for my audition for the national tour, and I got it. It was my dream come true. I will never forget my first rehearsal. I don't think I've ever been so nervous in my life, sitting between Angela Lansbury and George Hern, and in front of me, Hal Prince and Stephen Sondheim. After the year tour, I got to do the film for television.

A low point for me came right after that. When *Sweeney Todd* closed I still lived in Washington, D.C., so I had to move to New York. I had made the decision to do this for a living, now I had to go where the living was. I moved to New York and after I got the "bus and truck" tour of *Sweeney Todd*, I was unemployed for nine months. I was down to peanut butter and jelly. I finally took a full time job as a teacher at a private school and three months later, I was offered the lead in *Cats*. So I quit. I had to do it. I'm not a school teacher, I'm an actor.

When preparing for an audition, any actor who is putting himself on the line for musical theatre roles has got to stay in good shape. That means you have to study, vocalize every day, and practice. What would happen if you got a call for an audition and you hadn't opened your mouth to sing in three weeks? It isn't going to come out like you want it to. I found that I have to constantly keep myself in a state of being warmed up, ready to go. Spend about forty-five minutes in the morning warming up, go over your music, which also means you have to work with a pianist. You also have to work out exactly what you're going to say to the accompanist. It's very difficult to do a musical audition because many times, you will have to sit. You come in all warmed up, then you will have to sit and wait or talk to people. Then your nerves build. It's much easier when you get an agent, because you have a reserved time. The best way I can say to stay focused is to be very selfish. Don't visit with people, just sit someplace apart, keep your mind on what you're doing, go over the lines, and go in. If you're distracted by talking when they call your name, you may appear flustered. You don't want to present any of that; you want it to look like you're totally relaxed, and you've done this a million times. I think most auditioning is convincing the person on the other side of the table that they can trust you. When I auditioned for Hal Prince and Stephen Sondheim, they had to know that they could trust me with a $12 million dollar show. They had to know that they could trust me to give them what they needed eight times a week, at the same level, and not be a problem. It's all about trusting.

I couldn't get an audition for *The Phantom of the Opera*. The casting director said that Hal Prince said I wasn't right for the role. Well, I don't believe they ever asked him. Anyway, one of my friends was in *The Phantom of the Opera* in New York and he invited me to his New Year's Eve party. I knew if I went to that party there were going to be people there from the show. Within five minutes of walking in the door I had the audition. I had to get around the casting director. I know their job is very hard, and I don't mean to say that you always have to do that, but at the same time, I knew that I was right for that show.

The thing that keeps me going has changed over the years. In the beginning, I think a lot of it was that I had something to prove. Not only to my family and my friends, but to myself. After I did that, then it became more about leaving a legacy. When we filmed *Sweeney Todd*, I felt that enormously. I knew that I had really done something that will live on after me. For all time I will be in the original version of *Sweeney Todd*, and actors will base their characterization on that. I also feel now that I'm getting older, I'm able to give back some of the real honest opinions about the business. You can't sugar-coat it for actors. Actors have to be honest with themselves. One of my students was a waiter in New York for six years. He had come to New York to be an actor and had done a few little shows, but nothing much. Some of his friends from Atlanta called and asked him to become a founding member of a new theatre company there. He told me that he was having trouble with the decision. He felt that if he went back to Atlanta he would be a failure. I told him "But at the same time, you've been here six years, and nothing has happened. At least you will be happy and doing what you want to do." So he went to Atlanta, founded a theatre, and now it's a big theatre and he's doing very well. As for myself, I feel blessed that I've been able to make a living at something that I would have probably done for free.

WORDS OF ADVICE

- Be honest with yourself about your ability, your type, and know where you fit.

- If your singing is not that good, you've got to know it, get to a teacher, and develop yourself as far as you can go.
- The more experience and exposure you have, the more comfortable you will be.
- Push yourself to create original roles. If you can find new pieces, it will make your creative juices flow.
- Your frame of mind affects your work. Try to create an environment wherever you are that makes you happy. We get enough rejection in our lives and in our work; you should at least be in a living situation that is pleasant.
- For singing: find a teacher that communicates with you. You need that other ear to listen to you, particularly when you're younger. When you get older, your technique gets established. Just watch to make sure you don't fall into bad habits.
- There is a lot of stage fright that goes with singing, and meditation is very good for that.
- Do your research. Be knowledgeable about theatre. If you are auditioning for an Ibsen play, you need to know about the historical perspective of the time, about Ibsen's other works, and that he was the father of modern-day realism so that you play it in a style that is appropriate to the piece.

7

Ken Salley

Ken is forty-seven and originally from Brooklyn, New York. He has been pursuing acting for nine years. He trained at Los Angeles City College, West Coast Ensemble, and Odyssey Theatre, as well as in various workshops. His theatre credits include *A Midsummer Night's Dream* and *Troilus and Cressida*, both at the Globe Theatre. His film credits include *Night Falls on Manhattan*, *Mrs. Winterbourne*, and *The Preacher's Wife*. Ken's television credits include *Central Park West*, *New York Undercover*, and recurring roles on *General Hospital* and *Port Charles*. He appeared on a CD-ROM called *Turning Back the Clock*. He has also lent his voice to many educational radio workshops at WNYC. Ken received the Eastman Kodak International Amateur Film Award for producing and directing the short film *Ivory*.

When I was a kid I was a major film freak, and I still am. I would see movies on television and recreate them the next day in the schoolyard. My first acting experience came when I attended Brooklyn Technical High School. I was going to be an engineer, but I got bored with it. I realized I was more of an artist than an engineer. I loved science, but fortunately, we had the city radio station in our building. So, I got involved in the radio workshop. This was the same workshop where Barbra Streisand started several years before. It was acting, and it was my way of relieving stress and having fun.

For the past couple of years I supervised a telemarketing operation. We were selling subscriptions for the Pasadena Playhouse. We made it very actor-friendly. It was a place where actors could come and work, still pursue their goal, and not hide the fact that they were actors.

A highlight for me is what is happening right now. I'm going into a different age group and I'm getting response. I'm becoming the professional, older dad type, and I find a lot more jobs available to me. I just got my first voice-over job for a national ad as the warm and friendly type. I had been trying to break that barrier because I usually get picked right away for the announcer. Another highlight was that I got to model for a statue which is part of the Martin Luther King Memorial in Atlanta. The statues are seven marchers marching toward his tomb representing seven different parts of humanity in America, and I'm the first marcher.

A low point was when I lost my confidence. I took a sabbatical. I realized that I shouldn't be auditioning, because I didn't have the energy, and that extra special edge. I would show up, but I wasn't really showing up. There were other things I wanted to do in my life anyway, so I went out and did those. I let myself get excited about something else for a while. I really wasn't as organized about my career at that time as I am now. I wasn't networking, and I had vague goals, whereas now I have very specific goals.

When I arrived in New York, I got the bug again! Coming down the street at night and seeing the energy coming off of Broadway is ecstatic. There's a special kind of energy about being in a theatre or being on a set that you can't duplicate in other areas. I began to get in touch with the fun of it again, which had been missing.

The nice thing, now, is that they do use black actors for warm and friendly characters in commercials. They use black actors now for products that are not black-oriented. They weren't doing that fifteen years ago. There are still roles that I don't get, though. I notice a lack of love scenes for black romantic leads. Unless it's a Spike Lee film, there's still a hesitancy to show black men in a love scene.

I've had some auditions with casting directors and agents who treated me like I was their best friend, and it blew me away that they were so available to me. Then I have had auditions where they didn't even look at me for ten minutes because they were busy casting their other clients. If that happens, don't take it personally. Just re-focus on what you want to accomplish there. Think of something you want them to know about you that isn't on your resume. That will at least bring you back to a center point, because the casting director isn't there to make you comfortable. That's not their job, it's your job. I'm there to let this person know how we can form a partnership to create work for each other. They want me to do a good job, because if I do, they get paid and I get paid. My job is to be on target at least four out of five times.

I went in for an audition once that was just a two-minute slate of my name, but I felt a real good connection with the casting director. I didn't get that job, but a year later, I met the same casting director in a seminar. She remembered me and put me in a commercial.

Some of the ways I deal with rejection is by taking a walk, working out, or going to a dance class. I love African-Brazilian dance, and I will do that for a long time, get really sweaty, and let it go.

Having something personal to you that's happening in your life, whether it's acting or something else, can feed your career in ways that you can't expect. That's what's happening for me right now. I have a sense of calm, and I'm not desperate.

WORDS OF ADVICE

- Find out what's special about you. What can you do that nobody else can do?
- Have specific goals and a timetable for yourself.
- Look at the marketing end of this business in a serious manner.

8

Edward Tilghman

Edward is twenty-two, originally from Columbus, Indiana, but was raised in Connecticut. He's been pursuing acting actively for two years. He studied at the British American Drama Academy and Reed College. His theatre credits include *The Crucible, Rosencrantz and Guildenstern Are Dead, Three Sisters, Hamlet, Rumors, My Fair Lady*, and *Woman in Mind*. While continuing his acting pursuit, he has been a camp counselor for a summer drama camp, helping underprivileged children, and apprenticed at the Westport Country Playhouse for their Summer Stock Theatre as a technical intern. He also was production assistant for A. R. Gurney's play *Sylvia*, starring Stephanie Zimbalist and directed by John Tillinger.

It's the rush. I played sports, but it wasn't the same feeling as coming offstage. I love it. It's the rush more than anything else that pulled me into acting.

I'm doing an internship for the summer, but come October, I will be very unemployed. A friend of mine wants to make an independent film and he has the funds to do it. So, we are going to start that project soon.

A highlight for me was closing night of *The Crucible* playing John Proctor. The performance had gone very well, and I got off the stage to find my grandmother there. She had flown out just for my performance. I was shocked and surprised, and it was the first time she had seen me in a production.

A low point was my junior year of high school. I was asked to audition a lot, and the school put on twelve to fifteen shows a year. A lot were student directed and I couldn't say no. I tried to do three plays in my spring trimester. I got through the first show O.K., but by the time dress rehearsal week came, I was exhausted. I didn't have time to eat, and I couldn't remember a single line for the life of me. At dress rehearsal I was a total mess, and the next day I was told by the stage manager that I was no longer in the show. The director took my part. I was burned out, had lost twenty pounds, and then, they asked me to leave the school.

Before I get an agent, I'm going to work my ass off in Connecticut and build up my resume. If I can make it in Connecticut, I can make it in New York.

Theatre has been the one constant since ninth grade. Other parts of me have changed, but it's something that I know will stay. In order for me to live, I need to be involved in theatre. This is what happened; the first play that they took us to in London was the Royal Shakespeare Company's production of *Peer Gynt*. Alex Jennings was playing Peer Gynt. By the end of the performance, the girl next to me was crying and holding my hand, and we had only met a week before. I was crying, and we went out of the theatre in complete euphoria. At that moment, I thought, "If I ever have that kind of effect on an audience, or even one person, then it would have been worth it. I could die that day."

WORDS OF ADVICE

- When you get out of college, don't expect everyone to want you and love you. So where you can, make your own opportunities.
- No one will seek you out. Those fluke incidents where someone sees you in a restaurant don't happen. Don't rely too much on luck alone.
- I recommend going to London to study or doing an internship. They were the best decisions I ever made.

9

Luisa Di Capua

Luisa is thirty-four, and she is originally from Italy but grew up in Switzerland. She has been pursuing acting seriously for five years. She has studied at the Piero Dusa Acting Conservatory and with the Theatre of the Oppressed with Augusto Boal, among others. Her theatre credits include *Emily* at the Duality Playhouse, *Tales of a Hydrogen Starbomb* at the Sanford Meisner Theatre, *Election Year* at the New York Italian Theatre, *Candide* at the Sargent Theatre, *Beyond Therapy* at the Village Gate, and the narrator for a reading of *Heart of Darkness* with the Repertory Theatre. Luisa's film credits include *Skyride* and *Una Sera d'Estate* (Switzerland). She also records voice-overs for international commercials.

I'm very different now. I used to be shy and introverted, but in high school I always got the lead role in the play. People couldn't figure this out. Usually I wanted to blend in with the wall, but I loved being in a play because I could be somebody else. When I came to New York, I wanted desperately to find a way to come out of my shyness. I took a class called Acting For Non-Actors, which was more like public speaking, but there was some technique for emotional recall and improvisation. After a year, we had a scene study and performed it for friends and I was extremely nervous, but once the lights went up, and I did it, I thought: "I want to do this! I want to know more. I want to learn more."

I am lucky because I speak five languages and I'm a freelance interpreter. I am also doing temp jobs. Take an assessment of what your skills are and what they have to offer in a job.

I was doing a scene from *Who's Afraid of Virginia Woolf* for a showcase, playing Martha. The director kept telling me I had to be a bitch. It was really a stretch for me, because I'm not a bitch in real life. I told him I was being a bitch, but he said, "You're a nice bitch. It's not good enough." He told me "You have to find the animal in you." I didn't know what he meant. Then, scene night came, with the agents in the audience, and I was nervous. I was so mad at the director, because he had put this bug in my head and I couldn't get it out. I'm not sure to this day what happened, but we started the scene where my back was turned to my acting partner, and by the time I turned and addressed him, I had a look of such hatred, that he literally took a step backward. I scared him, and he told me this later. I'm not sure where it came from, but I found the animal. There was not a trace of Luisa during that scene, and I was ecstatic because I remember how I felt just before I went on. I was frustrated, mad at myself, the director, the world, and acting in general! To me, it was a gift. Afterward I went up to my director and said, "Did you like the animal?" He said, "It was there."

What I'm finding is that I get shut out of a lot of things because of my Italian dialect. They can't cast me for middle America. So I'm taking speech lessons for accent reduction. At this point my accent is a bigger problem than my look, so I'm working on that.

I acknowledge all of my fears and insecurities before I go into an audition. I know I'm nervous, and it's O.K. to be nervous, it's just energy. I know what I can do. I talk to myself, and remember that they are people just like me. I give myself a pep talk, acknowledge whatever is going on at that moment, and accept it as much as I can. If there is something that is really disturbing me, I say to myself, "I have a job to do right now, I promise I will get back to you in one half hour." It has worked pretty well for me.

I am freelancing with a couple of agencies from doing a showcase. I know a lot of people do mass mailings, but if you read up on the agents, you can tailor your short cover letter to whoever you're sending it to. For instance, if you find that an agency just moved into a new office, an entry line might be, "Congratulations on your new offices." Really personalize it as much as possible.

I have a philosophy that for every "yes" you have to hear one hundred "no"s. After I get depressed for a few minutes, I tell myself that I have added another "no" to my list and that means I'm getting closer to my "yes."

Every time I'm on stage for a performance, or even to rehearse, there is something magical about it. I feel fully alive. The process of finding a character is fascinating to me. It's fulfilling, and takes the whole of me into account—my body, intellect, and emotions.

WORDS OF ADVICE

- Network.
- Make contacts.
- We all want to make it, but it's also important to be true to yourself and not compromise your values. It's a big mountain to climb, but you want to get to the top in one piece with your integrity intact.

10

Tracy Bryce

Tracy is in her early thirties, originally from Illinois but grew up in California. She has been pursuing acting for fifteen years. She received her B.F.A. from U.C. Santa Barbara, and an M.F.A. from the University of Washington. She also studied at the London Academy of Music and Dramatic Art (LAMDA). Her theatre credits include *The Trojan Women, West Side Story, A Midsummer Night's Dream, Jesus Christ Superstar, East of Eden, The Glass Menagerie, Cabaret, Chicago, The Way of the World, The Duchess of Malfi, The Country Girl*, and *Macbeth*. Tracy's film and commercial credits include *The Goomba Brothers, Drugs on the Job*, and *Baby Contest*.

I always had excess energy. I started out singing and I was really loud, so they had to put me somewhere. So I sang in choirs. In high school I was going to be a doctor or lawyer, and I would act as a hobby. I went to a university that had a wonderful bachelors program in theatre. I think I must have secretly known that. I signed up for theatre as my major just on the premise that I could get into the classes. Two years later, I was completely engrossed. I kept pretending it was a hobby until I couldn't pretend anymore.

I'm making a living working at a retail store. My husband works as a waiter and bartender. You do need to have an actor-friendly job. For instance, I got a call-back, so I told my employer I couldn't be there on Friday, and it's O.K. because someone else is coming in for me. I'm also looking into teaching acting. I have an M.F.A. and that's one of the reasons I went to school, I can also teach. I want to start making my living at that while I'm pursuing my career.

Don't stay at any job that's tedious, makes you exhausted, or treats you badly. You don't want to be in a position where your morale is constantly battered down. You have to have that extra energy to do things for yourself and to pursue your career.

There's been a handful of highlights. I guess that's why we keep doing it, just for that handful. I had to do a graduate thesis before I graduated, and I decided it was time to write my own one-woman show. It's called *Suburban Trauma*. It's about growing up a white girl in the suburbs, where nothing really bad happens, but life is still hard anyway. It's about relative suffering. I wrote, directed, and performed it. I'm really proud of that, because it was all me. It was one of the times I felt a certain amount of authority in my field. I knew what I set out to do, and I achieved it.

It's really hard to be a woman in this business. There are fewer roles for us. I'm disappointed with how much harder I have to work because I'm a woman. Basically, I think there's a prejudice about women in our society. You're suppose to look a certain way, act a certain way, and if you don't, people don't know what to make of you. I've been accused of being too versatile, too changeable. In this business, it would be nice if people would look at women with the same breadth of vision with which they look at men.

When I'm preparing before an audition, I do yoga, breathe, and visualize what I want to do. I also let go at that moment right before-hand, and say it's O.K. It's all about concentration.

There was a big open call for a Broadway musical and I got there at 5:00 A.M. with a friend. We were already number 55 and 56 in line. Later on, there were thousands of people lined up. The auditions didn't start until 9:00, and we were there at 5:00. People had camped out overnight. When they finally got to audition us, they took us in groups of fifteen, and typed us out. The way they did that was by leading us through a system. Fifteen people went up an elevator at once. Then we got sent into a line, to wait to go into a room, to talk to someone at a desk, to give them our resume, to see whether or not we were going to be allowed to sing. So it was based on how we looked. This woman looked at my resume, which is filled with musicals, and she sort of nodded, until she saw that I attended LAMDA for a while. She asked me what I did there. I told her, "I sang and danced a little." She said, "Well, I guess we'll let you sing. Go ahead and take a ticket." The only reason I got in to sing was that this woman was turned on by my London credit, which was just a school training program. I have a lot more professional singing credits on my resume. So I got my ticket, and I swear to God it felt like Auschwitz. I went running down the hallway, breathing like crazy, and saw all these people, some with guitars, getting ready to go in. They had three studios going at the same time, with three different people watching. Instead of singing two songs that they had asked for, all they had time for was sixteen bars. So everyone had forty-five seconds to sing. I ran in, sang as fast as I could, and ran out. It was truly one of the most horrible experiences, and took me days to recover from the humiliation of that random typing out. Then, that frantic flight down the hallway thinking, "Am I going to the gas chamber or the work camp?" That's what it felt like. What completely blew me away, though, was that I got a call-back. Somehow that forty-five seconds of singing was O.K., but I felt like a wreck.

What keeps me going is that I've invested so much time and I love it so much. I've been doing it for too long, and there doesn't seem to be any going back.

WORDS OF ADVICE

- A lot of actors think they're just actors. They feel they can't write or direct, and they have to stay focused on acting. That's nonsense! You can do anything.
- Try to do all kinds of things that stimulate your creativity and keep you going on an artistic pursuit, even when you're not acting. That way, you're not dependent on someone telling you, "O.K., now you're allowed to be creative."
- If there's anything else you love to do, check that out as well. This business is a crazy-making way to exist, unless you feel that you would die without it.

11

Yassmin Alers

Yassmin is originally from New York and has been pursuing a theatrical career for five years. She studied at the
Academy of Dramatic Arts and the Herbert Berghoff studio. She performed in the Off-Broadway productions
Bring in the Morning and *Blocks*. She understudied Mrs.
Walker in the European premiere of *The Who's Tommy*,
and has done numerous industrials. She made her Broadway debut in *Rent*.

I had been pursuing a career in the recording field and it never took off.
So, for a change of pace and my own sanity, I decided to do something
else. That took me to musical theatre five years ago, and it's been a
successful five years.

I was able to make a living doing what I love to do, which is singing.
I sang with my own band in various nightclubs and at weddings. I
wasn't in the best scenarios at times, but at least I got to keep my voice
up and strengthen it. A lot of actors, dancers, and singers work the
front of the houses in Broadway theatres. They usher, or work the box
office, and bounce around from theatre to theatre. In fact, two of our
ushers for *Rent* got roles in the Boston production.

The highlight for me in my career is definitely being in *Rent*. I'm understudying, but I have been on for the lead several times. I decided that I wanted to be on Broadway a few years ago, and to actually see that dream come true was an amazing feeling—knowing that I had refocused my energy and accomplished my goal. My family was there to see me the first time I went on, and I just cried my eyes out after the show. It was a real emotional time for me and a very sweet experience, one I will never forget.

I could not be any happier to be young and ethnic right now. I think it's a great time for Hispanic actresses. I've waited a long time to see this market open us for us. I went through phases when I tried not to look Hispanic. Now it's in to be ethnic.

I once had a well-known director stop me on the street and tell me I had the next face that needed to be in pictures. There was an article in a magazine about his new movie. He bought me the magazine because he could see the look of disbelief on my face, being a New Yorker. I finally called him and we arranged to meet. We were supposed to meet at one place and he changed it, and all of a sudden I was meeting him at his hotel room. When I arrived, he started to tell me about all of the actors he has worked with. Then, he tells me about all the orgies that he's been involved in, and the men and women he's slept with. I guess he was trying to impress me, but all I wanted to do was get the hell out of that room. Needless to say, I just left. I never heard from him again.

I got my new agent through a friend. That seems to be the way in. I called her because I knew they were having auditions for *Rent* and the agent I had wasn't doing anything for me. So, when I called my new agent, I said "I'm going to get *Rent* and I need someone to submit me for auditions because I am right for this role." She knew I was serious and she had seen my work, so she submitted me.

I deal with rejection a lot better now than I ever have. I now walk in giving my best audition and then immediately turn it over to God when I'm done. Three years ago, I had five call-backs for the national tour of *The Who's Tommy* and I didn't get it. I was just a mess. I was so devastated that I could not see the show. I had to wait a year before seeing the show on Broadway. Then I auditioned for the European tour and my dance audition didn't go well, but Wayne Cilento, the choreographer, could see the desire in my eyes. I was able to let him know that I had been waiting a long time to be involved in this show. So, I redeemed myself when I got to sing. I understudied Mrs. Walker and went on for her many times.

I know that there's nothing else I would rather be doing. That's what keeps me going when I wake up in the morning. It's a means of expression, and I thank God for his faith in me.

WORDS OF ADVICE

- It helps if you're a triple threat. Learn to sing, dance, and act. You get a lot more work.
- After you send in a photo or leave a message on a machine, let it go. Turn it over to God's will.
- Don't go to the wrong auditions. If the part isn't right for you, don't waste your time. Be selective, or else you will waste your energy.
- When you go to an audition, walk in as if you already have the job.
- Don't meet strange men (or women) in hotel rooms, regardless of how legitimate they are. Meet in a public place.

12

Doug Blackburn

Doug is twenty-seven and has been pursuing acting since grade school. He is originally from Welch, West Virginia. He received his B.F.A. in theatre from West Virginia University and his M.F.A. from Carnegie Mellon University, which included a program at the Moscow Art Theatre School. He performed the role of Jackson Pollock in the Off-Broadway production *Jackson Pollock in the Painting*. In regional theatre he performed in *Waiting for Godot*, *The Fantasticks*, and he can be seen in a regional commercial for Blue Ridge Bank. He has recently performed the role of Jackson Pollock at the Rochester Institute of Technology with the National Deaf Theatre as artist in residence.

I went to West Virginia University and majored in English. The first year I was on academic probation and I thought I would be kicked out of school. So, I thought that acting had to be easy and decided to become an acting major. It wasn't easy. It was the hardest fun in the world. I don't mind dedicating sixteen hours a day to it because it's not work.

My first call-back was for a mid-season replacement for NBC. When I walked in I thought, "Oh, this is gonna be great," and when I walked out I thought, "Oh, this is gonna suck." For the past seven years

I had absolutely no rejection whatsoever. College was a real close, nurturing environment where if you failed, you got a pat on the back. It was nice, but it's not the real world.

By all means find a flexible job. I was always a good typist, so temp work was natural for me and I get along with new people easily. Whenever I need time off I say, "I can't work today," and it's fine with them. When I want to work, though, I call in and they give me a job. I can call in at 8:30 A.M. and I have a job at 10:00 A.M. If you can get a job where there's a word processor available, absolutely do it. In this day and age, actors need access to a computer for cover letters and updating resumes.

A highlight and breakthrough for me that is ongoing, is a one-hour performance art dance piece I perform called *Jackson Pollock in the Painting*. It's about the abstract artist Jackson Pollock. He created splatter painting using huge canvases on the floor. There are five dancers who play red, blue, black, white, and yellow. The idea is showing him at the easel saying, "I can't do this," to suddenly realizing "Wait a minute, let's paint on the floor and see what happens." It's about that split second, but it lasts an hour. It's like a dream. It's all set to jazz music and there's no speaking. Throughout the course of the show he paints with the dancers on stage, and it ends with florescent paint under strobe lights. I've been doing it for five years now, and for the rest of my life I will do this show.

When I'm sitting in a green room for an audition with thirty or forty people pushing up against the wall, I do crossword puzzles. I was very fortunate also to have a wonderful voice teacher, so I feel my voice is always there. I love a long, hot shower before I go to an audition. Physically, I go through my monologue a couple of times and remind myself of what my actions are, the beat changes, and what I want to do with it. I think one of the keys, though, is the voice. If one actor doesn't have the voice and another does, they will pick the actor with the voice.

Nothing gets me down. I just relax. The more weight I put on the rejection, the crazier I will drive myself. I know actors who moved to New York and are career waiters now. After two years of being beat over the head, they have drawn back, and they don't want it anymore. I'm not to that point yet, and I don't think that will ever happen to me. This is what I do. I refuse to let rejection bother me. It's just not worth it.

The thing that keeps me going is the thought: "Don't let the bastards get you down." The main thing I want in my life is to have fun. Once, I did an atrocious scene in summer school. It was the worst scene I had ever done, and afterwards, I realized I forgot to have fun. We re-worked the scene, did it three days later, and it was the best scene in the class. Fun is what drives me. This is fun.

WORDS OF ADVICE

- You have to spend money to make money. Acting is an expensive job. Make sure you have a source of money.
- When you have cover letters and headshots to send to agents, don't mail them in, deliver them.
- If you do want to mail them out, do it at the end of the week. Then they are on their desks Monday morning. You will get more phone calls that way.
- When picking out a day job, do something that makes you happy.
- Network with people. Keep in touch with people.
- Travel light. You have to be able to pick up and go wherever you are.
- Keep a support group around you, whether it's friends or family.
- Have some source of spirituality. Try to do one good thing for yourself everyday.
- Get your rest. Sleep is cheap, and it does help!

13

Max Ryan

Max is thirty-one, originally from Los Angeles, and has been pursuing acting for seven years. He trained at Los Angeles City College Theatre Academy and The Actor's Studio, among others. His theatre credits include *Noises Off*, *Hamlet*, *Ball Boys*, *Stage Door*, *The Merry Wives of Windsor*, *Sweet Charity*, *Hay Fever*, *West Side Story*, *Show Boat*, *The Matchmaker*, *A Midsummer Night's Dream*, and *You Can't Take It With You*. His film and television credits include *The Melting Pot*, *Soiree Sand Hors d'oeuvres*, *Exterminator II*, and *Kaiser Permanente Optical Video*.

When I was seven years old, my cousin, who was in college, babysat me and my ten-year-old sister. We stayed with her in her dorm room, and since she didn't know what to do with us, she took us to a play on campus. It was *Hamlet*, because I remember seeing the skull. I just loved it, and my sister and cousin hated it. At intermission they went outside and played, and I went back in to watch the rest of the play. I knew whatever it was that those people were doing, was what I was supposed to be doing. That was my first memory.

To help out with the bills, I cut hair. I didn't want to wait on tables. From doing theatre, I learned how to do make up and hair, and it was easy for me. I also went to hair school. That's one of the best things I ever did, because it's always gotten me through. When I was at my acting academy, once a month students would go into the green room and I would cut their hair for $5 or $10 each, whatever they could give me. I survived on that. Now I know I can support myself as an actor because a few things have worked for me. I don't want to give up cutting hair completely, but it's a false security. A lot of people have other careers *and* their acting, but that becomes false security. It doesn't make you go out there and say "I've got to go!"

A highlight for me was the show *Noises Off.* It was one of the biggest roles I've ever had, because I've always played smaller character roles. The physical comedy was hard, and it was my first show moving away from my safe, secure environment of Los Angeles. I got that show on my fourth audition in New York, and that was great. Also, something inside of me changed deeply, and I knew I was much more of an actor. It was a combination of things in my life, the role, and the response from the audience. In my comedy acting, I played at things a lot. I would show, show, show, and I've always had success doing that. I've learned as I've gotten older that the only way to really act is to be in the moment—no matter what it is, heavy drama or extreme physical comedy. I would always approach drama trying to be in the moment, but in comedy, I knew the shtick, the timing, and I knew what to do to get laughs. In this role, however, I was very instinctual, organic, and real.

A low point for me was an audition. I auditioned for *Little Shop of Horrors.* I knew I could do the role, but I hadn't been working on my voice. I brought a little plant with me to put on the piano and I was going to sing "Grow For Me." The actor before me did the same song, brought a plant, put it on the piano just as I was going to do, and he was excellent. He had the voice. I flipped out, because I've done musical auditions before, but they scare me. I went in and choked up. I started to sing and nothing came out. They told me I could start again, I got two lines into the song, and choked up again. I said "I have to go now. This isn't a good day for me." So I picked up my little plant and walked out of that room. I was so humiliated, beyond crying. It taught me a great lesson: never go if you don't think you're prepared. If you ever have a doubt, don't go!

Every audition is different. I've found a whole new way to prepare.

Since I've been in New York, I started taking a class for the technique of being in the moment and never trying to be something I'm not. It really got me in touch with being here and being now. The more I try to deny something, the more it's going to persist. So instead of trying to relax all the time, I just go with what I'm feeling at that moment. If the audition is a straight acting piece, I do an intense meditation and I run. Those two things help me to be centered and connected to my impulses. I also don't try too much to be the character. I try to be a blend of me and the character. Many times I would try to be the character and deny who I was, and deny my own impulses. Now, I've learned how to be me, then the character comes, and I find the middle. I'm a real good imitator, but I didn't process it completely through *me* first.

About rejection; it depends on the day. It depends on where my head's at. I was too emotionally involved before, but now, I see it as a business. My logo may not fit with someone's product, but it eventually will somewhere else.

What keeps me going is the thought of not doing it. Every time I've wrestled with the thought, "Do I want to keep doing this?" I was miserable. So I can't *not* do it. There's a reaching-out in my soul that keeps me wanting to communicate on that level with people. Acting is the only way I can see to do that. I want to affect people's lives, and that's what keeps pulling me toward acting.

WORDS OF ADVICE

- Don't listen to the world. They will keep telling you you're supposed to fit in, get the car and the house. It's not that you can't have those things, but if you're really an actor, believe those things will come and don't deny following your heart.
- Keep your focus, but take it easy on yourself. When the time is right, you will have your moment. Don't feel guilty if you're not working every day.

14

Shelby Rose

Shelby is in her twenties, originally from Southern California, and has been pursuing acting in New York for four years. She graduated from Boston Conservatory with a B.F.A. and continues vocal, dance, and acting training in New York. Her New York and regional theatre credits include *How To Succeed in Business Without Really Trying*, *Oklahoma!*, *The Importance of Being Earnest*, *No, No, Nanette*, *Meet Me in St. Louis*, *Cat on a Hot Tin Roof*, *The Seagull*, and *The Heidi Chronicles*. She also performed national tours of *A Christmas Carol* and *Babes in Toyland*.

I originally started out studying opera. A friend talked me into going to an audition for a graduate-directed play simply as moral support for him. I wasn't even planning on auditioning, but they offered me Hermia in *A Midsummer Night's Dream* and I turned it down. I said, "I'm not an actor," but the director talked me into doing it. I loved it, and the bug bit me. It was completely unintended.

I've been waiting tables for ninety percent of my income because it's the most convenient. I wish I could say it was from acting. It will be from acting. But right now, it's waiting tables. Most actors wait tables, but if you can find something that you do well, most definitely do it, because waiting tables is very stressful. Especially if you make good money, because you can get caught up in it and lose perspective.

Just about every acting job I've done has been a highlight for me, because I learned so much from every one. Everything I've been involved in has been a wonderful learning experience for me and helped me grow.

I was unemployed when I made the transition from Non-Equity actor to Equity-Eligible. So I had a little over a year of just waiting tables. I was auditioning like crazy, and auditioning very well. I was also in class and growing as an actor, but not working. That was really hard, because I heard that little voice in my head say "What if you never work again?" The most important thing was my support, the people behind me who helped me.

Before an audition, I keep quiet, keep to myself, keep focused, and I breathe, because I forget to breathe. It's kind of funny, but I do. I focus on breathing and being alert to what's around me, and make sure that my audition material is ready to go. Another thing I do before I go in, is to read a card that a friend gave me about self-worth and believing in yourself. It gives me a glow inside and makes me feel like I'm special, because we all are. It's hard to remember that when you're at an audition where 350 people want it just as badly as you do. I tell myself that I'm special, I have a gift, and I'm going to go in and share it with them. That always helps me to do my best.

The first professional job I got, I went in, sang for them, and they liked me. Then they wanted to see my dancing, but they didn't have the choreographer there. So they told me to just do something "ballet." They played some music and said "Just do something." Then they told me to do something "jazz." It was the weirdest situation. There I was improvising dance steps. I've never experienced anything like it since. I wasn't even in dance clothes, I was in a skirt and heels.

I think it's really important to get an agent who believes in you, will send you out, and will work hard for you. Remember that they work for you, and not the other way around. I've experienced a philosophy among some agents, where it seems they feel they have a certain power. In a way they do, but it's really about the actor. That's why it's important to find someone who believes in the actor, cares about the actor, and wants to work with the actor to create a career. It's about the long haul, and not just about the paper signed.

Rejection is not a rejection about my talent, it's always about type. If I don't get it, they might have hired someone they've already worked with. It's about connections, and type. I audition a lot, because if I have one audition in a week, it's harder to walk away from than if I've had seven.

What keeps me going is that I love it like nothing else. It gets me through the dark times, too, because when I do get a job, and I'm working, it inspires me. It reminds me of why I got involved in the first place. I love the work. I also love the classes, and working toward the work.

WORDS OF ADVICE

- It's all about self-worth and persistence.
- It's very important to keep your skills sharp and your feet wet.
- It doesn't matter if people in school said certain actors would be the next stars and other actors would never make it. That's something I feel they never had the right to say. Just work on your craft and love it, because that's why you're doing it.

15

Trevor Wallace

Trevor is in his early forties and has been pursuing acting for ten years. He is originally from New York and studied acting at the Harlem School of the Arts. On stage he has performed in *I Heard About Your Cat*, with the National Black Theatre, *Gift of Life*, at Cami Hall, *Adventures with Rico*, and *Purlie Victorious*, both at the Harlem School of the Arts. His film credits include *The Professionals*, *King of New York*, *The Warriors*, and *Moscow on the Hudson*, directed by Paul Mazursky. On television he appeared on *Kojak* and filmed a pilot for a series called *The War Room*. Trevor has also appeared on *All My Children*, *Another World*, *One Life to Live*, *Ryan's Hope*, and *New York Most Wanted*. He has also done commercials for British Airways, NY Telephone, Country Time Lemonade, and Fastrack Sneakers.

Part of what got me started was when the movie *The Learning Tree* came out and everybody asked if I was in the movie. I looked like one of the actors in the film and it gave me a good feeling. Then one of my friends saw a photograph of me and said that I should be a model. So I started modeling. From there I bounced off to theatre. My friend told me if I wanted to do theatre, I had to start training and learn. So, I studied with Dorothy Maynard at the Harlem School of the Arts. She was the first black opera singer. She took a group of us and taught us all aspects of the theatre. When they tore the school down to build a new one was when we all went our separate ways.

I make my living now from acting, and when I need to, I collect unemployment. I have my own house, and three children. It's a struggle. Whatever money I make, I put in the bank. I used to work at an engineering company, and one year everyone got a raise except me. That helped me decide that I wanted to continue in acting because that's where I felt more appreciated, and that was what I loved to do. When you feel more confident and know the roots of this business, then you will make that transition to full-time acting. Don't force anything, because everything will come naturally.

When I audition I try not to gossip. I want to keep a clear head, stay focused, and be me. I try to see the character, what he's doing, and get that into my head. Also, I always have a backup strategy ready for approaching the character in case they want to see it another way.

A lot of actors have a heavy theatrical background, and that's where I need to get more strength. I'm established in SAG, so now I want to go in another direction, go back to basics, and that's theatre. The people with theatrical background carry more weight. I think the opportunities are good for black actors right now as well, because parts are busting out all over.

I got my agent from mailing out my picture and resume. To get an agent is difficult and easy at the same time. I learned by going to a lot of seminars where agents came in and told us what they like and what they don't like. Most of the time they said you need a good picture. You have to handle rejection or else you'll find yourself walking across the freeway. I remember one actor wanted attention, so he went to the Brooklyn Bridge and said he was going to jump. That's carrying it a little too far!

My friend's nephew came up with an interesting idea. He went to Los Angeles, is already in the union, and has been cast in different roles. Every time he gets a job, he puts his picture in a balloon, sends it to the casting people, and thanks them. That's his own little gimmick. They always call him, and that's how he started getting parts. You have to come up with something original for yourself. It all depends on you.

WORDS OF ADVICE

- Be real. Be who you are.
- Be patient and stay focused.
- Learn your craft. At this point they don't need you, you need them.
- If you are rejected, move on to the next audition, because the next part may be yours.
- Don't rush anything, take your time. Get your union cards and then go to the next level.
- Keep your ears open, communicate, network with people, and always be polite.
- Listen to people with experience, because their experience will help you grow. Then you can pass on what you know to the actor coming behind you and get satisfaction from it.

16

Leanne Whitney

Leanne is twenty-four, and has been pursuing acting for three years. She is originally from Boston, and she has studied at various studios in New York. Her film credits include *Celtic Pride*, *Hunger Strike*, *Seulement Un Café*, and *Minds-On Science*. She also appeared in commercials for Mitsubishi and Windsor Savings Bank. Her theatre credits include *Reflections*, *Rebel Without a Handbag*, and *Angela's Bachelorette Party* (Boston Showcase Production).

After I graduated from college, I started working for my father in sales. In business, the opportunity to make a lot of money was there, but there was no form of creativity. After a few months, I realized I wanted to be in the arts instead of business. I knew that the arts were harder to pursue and become successful in, but that's where my heart was. So, I kept working as I started training, and more and more, I realized I had to do this.

I still work for my father. I do his books on computer. I'm lucky that I can work my own hours because I can log on from my computer. I think getting a job is really important; otherwise, it gets too depressing being a "starving artist."

I'm in a play called *Reflections*, and we travel to colleges and schools in the northeast. The play is about anorexia. The script if so moving and powerful, it makes my hair stand on end at the end of each performance. The Massachusetts Eating Disorder Association produces it, but it's a shame we don't have more performance dates, because it's a brilliant piece of work. The actors in the cast are so talented, every time I do a performance, it's a highlight. It's so rewarding because we are helping people at the same time. The playwright was hospitalized for anorexia, and some of her friends have died from it, so, she speaks to the students before each performance. It's an important piece, and we have gotten phenomenal response.

I had the best course in rejection. One summer during college, I sold books door to door. You don't get harsher rejection than that. Every actor should go out and do a door-to-door sales job, because when you get those doors slammed in your face, the rejection in this business seems minor. Every now and then, I let the rejection bother me. That's really my only low point, because I love going after this profession. Monday through Friday I'm auditioning, trying to make connections, and I study. Then I work on Saturday and Sunday. Sometimes I have no social life. After a couple of months, if I haven't allowed myself to relax, rejection starts to eat at me. I just have to go away for a few days to remind myself that I have another life, a great family, and that this isn't the only thing that I'm about. That's my outlet.

When preparing for an audition, I think relaxation is ninety-eight percent of the job. If you can relax into it, and let the emotion come out through what you're saying, it makes all the difference in the world. If I have a few moments before I go into the audition room, I stretch, breathe deep, and relax to get the tension away.

I went to an audition for an Equity play. I got there at 4:25, and my appointment was at 4:30. The 4:45 appointment got there before me, and a friend dropped me off. Well, there was an older woman signing people in, and she had let the 4:45 auditioner in ahead of me. I told her that my call time was 4:30, and that I really had to go at my call time, because someone was waiting for me. She had already given the director the order of auditioners showing me coming after the person she let in early. I don't know what she said to him, but, when I got in there, he didn't listen to a word I said. He didn't say hello, or introduce himself. He flipped through pages, and didn't look at me during the whole audition. I could tell he just wanted me to do my thing and leave. I was so mad, because I had bought the play and prepared for that audition.

There's a great place here in New York called The Actor's Connection. You have to pay, of course, but a lot of casting directors and agents go to see the showcases. It's run by an acting couple, and they've been in the business for years, so a lot of the agents that come are friends of theirs. It's $20, and you can sign up for what you'd like to showcase for, be it commercial copy, monologues, songs, or soap copy.

What keeps me going in acting is that through another voice, I am able to live a range of human emotions in a short period of time. I get to bring people with me on that trip, and hopefully, have them access that emotional experience with me.

WORDS OF ADVICE

- It's good to start somewhere smaller like I did in Boston. The markets are smaller, so try to book some acting jobs and have them on your resume when you get to Los Angeles or New York. That way you will have experience.
- Constant training is really important so that you are fresh when that call comes in. By staying in class, you also meet people who are in the same boat as you and develop your skills.
- You have to be patient and prepared to do it.
- You have to understand the sales side of the business. In all sales, it's the law of averages. The more people see you, the better. Someone's bound to like you and cast you in something.
- You have to be able to present yourself. You can't just be a great actor and have no rapport with an agent. It isn't just your ability, you are the whole package.

17

Colleen Davie

Colleen is twenty-seven and originally from Nashville, Tennessee. She has been pursuing professional acting for two years. She received her B.S. in Broadcasting from Boston University and continued with acting training in New York. Colleen's theatre credits, among others, include *The Undoing, Lenny, Nothing in Common*, as well as *True Love* at the Douglas Fairbanks Theatre, *Murder on Center Stage*, and *Meet Me in St. Louis*. Her film credits include *JFK* and independent shorts such as *Hand In Hand, Office Wars, Directions*, and *The Secretary*.

The person that made me decide to pursue acting was Harrison Ford. I saw *Star Wars* when it came out on cable. The final scene when Harrison Ford receives his medal and winks at Princess Leia made me cry. He made me feel something. I decided that I wanted to do what he was doing. To affect people as he had affected me. That is the one thing that has kept me going. I did finally meet him on the set of *Sabrina* where I worked production, and I thanked him for inspiring me. I told him "I hope to be in a movie with you one day." He said, "I wish you luck." I said, "Thank you very much. I'll be seeing you soon."

I worked in film production for four years and then had to drop out completely and start turning down all production work, because when I got behind the camera and watched the actors, there was a burning desire to be where they were. It became hard to watch. I now do temp work. If you have any computer skills you can make really good money as an administrative assistant. What I find great about temping is that it's flexible, and if you have an audition or a job, you call them up and tell them you can't come in the next day. I did have to call an agency recently to tell them I couldn't take a job and they became mad. They called me back, telling me that I had made them look bad, and I said, "I told you four years ago that I'm an actor first and that is my priority." So you have to be careful and meet *your* needs first, because if you go out of your way too much, people will walk all over you.

A highlight for me was the closing night of *Lenny*. It was the most incredible feeling in a performance that I've ever had. The audience was excellent and the energy was great. We had a limited engagement of three weekends and we packed the house every night. Sometimes, when I've gone to little Off-Off-Broadway shows, I've seen lots of empty seats in the house and I would think "God, no one knew about this show." For *Lenny*, we weren't allowed to list the show or have reviews, and we still packed the house. It was a great feeling to know that we could bring people in. The highlight of my training was the moment I was able to cry on stage. To find the ability to call it up at any time I wanted. I found a way to reach in and touch it.

A low point for me was an experience I had with a teacher. I wanted to study a particular acting method and I could not afford the classes. So I had to look around for studios that would let me work for half of my tuition, and I found one. The guy was suave, cool, and he was passionate about teaching. I learned a tremendous amount and grew a lot from it, but as the second year came, he was concentrating on moving to Los Angeles. So I was helping him in the office and on my computer at home. I ended up helping more than I had to because he was very manipulative, and he could talk people into anything. I don't care how smart I was or how aware I was of what he was doing, it was hard to take a step back and say "I know who this man is. Stop being taken in." He used my generosity, my ability on the computer, and my office position so much, that by the time it was over, I almost hated the man. I could not learn from him anymore because he had abused my trust. His mind was in Los Angeles three months before his body was and we had a showcase coming up. He was not trying to help us, he was just going through the motions.

In terms of auditions, don't give them the power. *Never* give over the power. You are in control of everything, and remember, they *want* you to be the one they cast. They don't want to go through a million other people. I have a friend who recently lost his entire family in a plane crash. In a sense, he has nothing to lose now. So when he goes into an audition, he doesn't care what they think about him. He has booked more acting jobs in the last six months than you could ever believe. He has a different perspective on life. We live 30,000 days on the average, and that is short. Take a step back, and look at auditioners as just people, remembering that they have no control over you.

Rejection doesn't matter. Once I walk out of an audition, I take ten minutes and go over it in my mind, and then I forget it. Actually, I don't even consider it a rejection, they just didn't call me. If I walk out and I don't feel good, I will pick up *Backstage*, or go to SAG, and I'll start looking up the next audition. I will also go through the *Hollywood Reporter* and read about what other actors are doing or I will go to a movie, because I'm always inspired when I go to a movie.

What keeps me going is the fact that every morning when I wake up, acting is the first thing I think about, and I think about it all day long. When I'm typing up letters in an office, I'm thinking about acting jobs and where I'm going to be. It's the *only* thing I want to do. I think of it in this way: If I said "I don't want to act, I think I want to own the Deutsch Bank," then, I know that one day I would own the Deutsch Bank, because that's what I set my mind to do. So if I am smart enough and strong enough to own the Deutsch Bank, why the hell can't I get a job in a movie? It's just as hard. If you have *one* goal, then there's only *one* result possible: that you will achieve it.

WORDS OF ADVICE

- If you want it badly enough, you can have it.
- Don't trust everybody.
- When you're working, don't tell people about your private life. Remember that it's a business, and your private life doesn't come into the business unless a director asks what touches you for the development of a character. That's the moment that your private life can come into it, but at no other time.

18

Philip J. Mastrelli

Philip is fifty-five, originally from New York, and has been pursuing acting for thirty-five years. Philip's regional theatre credits include *Dames at Sea*, *Mame*, *Musical Comedy Murders of 1940*, *Social Security*, *The Boyfriend*, *Twice Around the Park*, *Lovers and Other Strangers*, *Company*, *Once Upon a Mattress*, and *Anything Goes*. In dinner theatre he has performed in *I Do, I Do*, *A View from the Bridge*, *Fiddler on the Roof*, *Catch Me If You Can*, and *A Funny Thing Happened on the Way to the Forum*. His television credits include *Edge of Night*, *Poor Man Blues* (cable), *New York News*, and *Central Park West*. In film, Philip's credits include *Eraser*, *Sleepers*, *First Wives Club*, *The Devil's Own*, and *Ransom*.

When I was seven years old, I had the opportunity to see the tail end of Vaudeville. At the end of the feature at the Loew's 86th Street movie theatre in Manhattan, there would be a variety stage show, and I remember how I couldn't wait to hear the live orchestra start to play its theme as the sheer, glittery show curtain parted and the emcee appeared in the brightest, whitest spotlight. I knew then how much I loved theatre. I always knew I was a creative person and very musical. As a kid,

I was always chosen to play leading roles in my grammar school plays and I choreographed dance routines in my parent's living room to the music being played on the radio. However, I never thought that I would become an actor, because I was brought up in a very traditional family, with traditional values. Mom and dad were of Italian extraction, and their generation believed you grew up, got educated, and sought out job security by working for the city, state, or federal government and continued on the path to lifetime stability by getting married and providing them with grandchildren. That was it! I was never given acting, dancing, or singing lessons as a child. My parents never encouraged acting as a profession, because I'm sure they thought that singing and dancing were things you did for fun, and actors were discovered à la Lana Turner and not trained professionals. I became more aware of acting as a profession in college. I found it very fulfilling and I was very happy doing it. Although I worked toward a B.A. in advertising, I didn't further my studies in my major, nor did I seek a job in that field. The acting bug had taken hold of me!

When I first started acting, I was married and working for a major airline on a full-time basis. It was a flexible job in that I could swap hours and days off with other employees. So, aspiring actors might consider an airline job, since they could feasibly get the time off they need to pursue their craft, pending the airline's swapping policies. Later on, I voluntarily switched to part-time to afford more time to pursue acting, and acting-related professions. My ex-wife and I became talent managers. I found that discovering and coaching new, young talent was equally as rewarding as performing. We were successful inasmuch as we developed a couple of newcomers who went on to appear in soap operas, television, feature films, and Broadway.

Now, as I continue to pursue acting, I still try to do work that's as flexible as possible to allow time for auditions. Most of these jobs are seasonal or temp. I've done convention work, and gift shows, been an airport meeter/greeter, and had great fun as a mystery shopper, which is actually acting-related. You get to perform, because you impersonate a consumer. One of the main clients I was shopping for was a bank. I would observe the facility and its employees, investigate their procedures, what they had to offer, and ultimately write a report.

Another job actors should consider is proofreading. The hourly rate starts at $12 and up. Although, it may seem a tedious job, it's something you can do in off hours. I know actors who have been doing it for thirteen years on a freelance basis, and it allows them to go to auditions, and to have time for acting jobs. Another suggestion might be to first focus on commercial acting. Once you land a long-running, national commercial especially, you can earn the money you need to free you up to do other work which may not pay as well, such as theatre.

In my pursuit of acting, I don't know of any one special highlight, except for the feeling I get from performing in front of a live audience and hearing that applause. For me, it's an electric, exhilarating experience. *It makes me feel energized, and I love it.* I remember back in college, some stranger and his wife came up to me and said, "That was such a great job, you should be on Broadway." That encouragement carried me through, as did a number of compliments from a voice-over teacher who said, "You're either a good actor, or a good liar." I know they're just words of encouragement, or maybe the affirmation an actor always seems to be seeking, but their words were highlights for me.

A low point for me was my lack of confidence at the outset. Because of being raised in a family that didn't support this kind of profession, or lifestyle, I didn't know if I had the stuff to be a professional actor. Even in college I was discouraged when, in a journalism class, a professor told us that anyone who opens a newspaper and turns to the theatre section first is hopeless, a goner, and lost forever! Certainly, that statement, as narrow a view as I know it to be today, did little to bolster my confidence, and every actor needs confidence building at some point.

Toward that end, your representation can help you. I deal with a personal manager. Being a former talent manager, I feel a manager gives you more personal attention, has your best interests at heart, doesn't have as many actors in his stable (as does an agent), or as many actors in your category. Therefore, you should get submitted for more auditions. Ultimately, you will sign with an agent, because that's the nature of the business. The positive in this is that you have two people going to bat for you. In this business, surrounding yourself with supportive people and confidence builders is imperative!

What keeps me going are the words of encouragement I receive from fellow actors and directors, and the occasional applause. Everyone wants to go to a job they're going to be happy in, no matter what they're doing. The happy feeling I get from performing never leaves me. It makes me want to continue, and the recognition I receive for a job well done is just icing on the cake!

WORDS OF ADVICE

- Pursue acting for all the right reasons: fulfillment and satisfaction. Forget the glamour, the fame, and the anticipated millions, because it could be a long road.
- Know the business of the business. Be aware that it is a business and that you are a commodity.
- You can't leave the marketing effort to your agent or manager alone, you must market yourself.
- There are many books and videotapes on the market if you can't afford any of the acting-related or business-related seminars or workshops.
- Get involved with reputable theatre groups when doing Off-Off Broadway work.
- The trade papers are an excellent source for jobs, acting and otherwise.
- Sometimes the networks have open auditions for soap operas. Contact each of them to find out when they are held, and send your picture to them periodically.
- On a more specific note, you can further enhance your commercial acting skills if you read the copy in magazine and newspaper ads and on cereal boxes out loud as if you were doing a commercial, and try several different deliveries.
- Obtain a Ross Report (a small monthly publication containing up-to-date agent and casting director listings).
- If you're a member of the acting unions, avail yourself to all the free, or nearly free, seminars given by directors, producers, casting directors, agents, and fellow actors.

19

Abiola Abrams

Abiola plays an age range of eighteen to twenty-five, is originally from New York, and has been pursuing acting for three years. She received her B.F.A. from Sarah Lawrence College and continued with classes in New York. Her film credits include many independent films in addition to work on *Central Park West*, *Crossings*, and *The Nanny*. Television appearances include video jockey work here and in Japan on shows such as *USA Live*, and *MTV Jams*. Her theatre credits include *Giovanni's Room* and *The Panthers*, a one-woman play performed at the International African Arts Festival. She feels that her most important work to date has been creating a performance group with two other actresses called Goddess City.

When I was in high school I was a rapper. I always wanted to be on stage, in the productions going on at school, but my self-esteem wasn't high enough to make me audition. I would prepare a piece and then not show up. When I got to college, I felt more comfortable with being myself, so I started performing my own poetry. I felt the rush of being on stage and realized the words on the page were nothing until I brought life to them. Bringing life to another person that's just on paper made me decide there was nothing else I would rather be doing. My second major in school was creative writing, so I'm a writer as well. Of course, creative writing doesn't pay the bills yet either, but I do a lot of proofreading, copyediting, and cosmetic copyrighting to help me financially. My family is also incredibly supportive, and I still live with my parents. I know that pursuing acting is a sacrifice I'm making, so I don't ask them for too much because they shouldn't have to make a sacrifice; this is my sacrifice.

A highlight for me was when I came back to New York after an upsetting interview with a Los Angeles talent agent who advised me to "Get out of the business, you're beautiful and talented, but so is everyone else. There's no work besides the sexy girlfriend." Well, after that, I decided to give life to a project that I'd been working on for a year. My goal was to create a performance group that would bring my generation to the theatre, and give a voice to the voiceless folks who look just like us that we pass on the subway or in the park everyday. I needed collaborators who were also leaders and knew exactly who to call. It was a cold day on the set of yet another groovy music video when talented, well-trained actresses were told to bump and grind in a tub of pudding. Fuming, I marched out and only two other actresses left with me. Guess who I called?

I took matters into my own hands to create work that I felt was worthy of me. The project is called Goddess City, and it is where we realize that we control our own destinies, unapologetically. We have the nerve to tell the truth about the fever inside that inspires us. Goddess City is a production offering theatrics, spoken songs, and an exciting blend of hip-hop, funk, reggae, and R&B music. We premiered in North Carolina at the National Black Theatre Festival, a week-long international celebration. The show is a journey to Goddess City, the capitol of self-esteem. We aim to change the way people view theatre.

I was in an interview with an agent once, and she asked me who I thought was getting my roles out there in the industry. I told her Neve Campbell and Lisa Kudrow. She was a little disturbed that I didn't name African-American actors. Then she asked, "Well, name some black actresses," so I did. The first two names I gave her, though, are the actresses who are doing roles I feel I could play, and just because they're white and I'm black doesn't mean I can't relate to them. That was strange. On the surface, it looks like it's come really far, but there are a lot of issues that need to be worked out. I think it will come with this new generation of actors that will hopefully take it to the next level.

When I was looking for an agent, I went to One On One productions. They have a listing every month of casting directors and agents who are going to be their guests. You get fifteen minutes alone with them. A lot of places offer this kind of service also for a fee, but what makes this one special is that you have to audition to be a part of the group. Agents know that, so they prefer coming to a place with pre-screened talent. Through them, I started freelancing with an agency and then went on a quest for the perfect headshot! I finally got a good one, started being called in for more auditions, and signed with the agency. When interviewing agents my main question to them is: "If it doesn't say 'black female' in the character breakdown, will you submit me for the role if you believe I can do it?" I have friends who have agents that do fight for them to get into auditions that are not specifically for black roles.

The first thing I do to prepare for an audition is to make sure I have a destination after the audition. I go to the gym, or have dinner with a friend, so that my focus isn't completely on it. When I get to the audition, I try to talk to as few people as possible, because that diffuses my energy. I just let people know that I can catch up with them later, but at that moment I have to stay in character and maintain what I've worked on. I also think about myself in the situation of the scene. If this were to happen to me, what would I be telling my friend or mother about it. I do that to get into the character and make it more real for me. The last thing I do is create a very strong moment before. Whatever happened to the character just before the scene takes place, I make real inside my head. Then I begin, and also bring a positive energy into the room. The chances to perform are so seldom that I look forward to performing and I enjoy it.

What keeps me going is knowing what I'm working toward. As an artist, I consider myself a public servant. This is what I have to offer, and the reason I'm doing it is because I know all things are truly possible. There may be two people who are going through the same experiences, and one person may end up begging on the corner, and the other will end up Oprah Winfrey. Just having that willpower and persistence is so important. It's the last person standing! If you quit, who's to say that the very next day couldn't have been the day you got that incredible role. I have absolute faith. So many opportunities and wonderful people have come my way that the positives outweigh the negatives. So when I wake up in the morning and think "It's another day of mailing out the headshots and getting the trade papers," I know that doing these things is an essential component. Being aware of the business aspect keeps you ahead and will ultimately distinguish you.

WORDS OF ADVICE

- My agent makes 10 percent, which means I have to do 90 percent of the work.
- While you're waiting on line for an audition, don't waste your time. Read a book about acting or the industry to increase your knowledge.
- It's up to us to go out there and break the boundaries and not believe that a new idea is impossible just because no one has done it before. Create your own work.
- Stay away from all negative thinking and negative people because it's infectious and gets under your skin, but positive thinking is infectious as well.
- Stay centered and have faith.
- Do your research.
- Spend time in bookstores reading biographies of actors, and get books on how to be a working actor. For instance, you wouldn't go into a dry-cleaning business without finding out what other drycleaners have done to start their business.
- Keep a journal.
- Don't ever feel like you have to sit at home waiting for the phone to ring. If you were working at a regular job, you would be in an office for eight hours a day, so give at least half that time to pursuing acting. That may be sending a mailing of pictures and resumes, or making phone calls for further contacts, or meeting people.
- Come to enjoy the business aspect of acting. It's a very real part of it.

20

June Angela

Originally from New York, June has been acting since age five. She graduated with a B.A. in Performing Arts at eighteen and has trained with acting teachers in New York. June received both Tony Award and Drama Desk Award nominations as Best Leading Actress in a Broadway musical for her starring role as Mariko in *Shogun*. Her numerous credits include co-starring as Tuptim in the Broadway and London revivals of *The King and I* with Yul Brynner and *Lovely Ladies, Kind Gentlemen*, her Broadway debut. Off-Broadway, she starred in works at Lincoln Center, New York Shakespeare Festival, and Pan Asian Repertory, where she received critical acclaim for her lead performance in the world premiere epic *Cambodia Agonistes*. On television she was a regular on *Mr. T & Tina* (ABC) with Pat Morita and *The Electric Company* (PBS) with Bill Cosby, for which she received an Emmy Award of Honor and a Grammy Award. June was invited to star in the world premiere musical *Sing to the Dawn*, which was chosen to open the 1996 Festival of the Arts in Singapore, and she can be heard on the original-cast CD recording. She is a recurring villain on the cartoon series *The Real Adventures of Jonny Quest* and does numerous voices for Disney as well.

When my brother was born, my mother shared her hospital room with an English actress who saw me and made my parents promise to take me to a modeling agency. That's how I got started. I modeled as a child and started appearing in commercials. My parents had three things that I had to follow in order for me to continue in show business. First, if I didn't like what I was doing, they would never force me. Second, my schoolwork was very important, and I had to keep up my grades. The third thing was, if I turned into one of those stage brats that they had heard of, out I would go!

I have been very fortunate, because I've been able to make my living totally in the arts, and I am grateful for that. However, if you need an outside job to support your craft, I would recommend a job that doesn't take up all of your time. It could also be helpful to have your own business as a sideline. I know actors who own consulting firms and can make their own hours.

Definitely a highlight for me was getting the Tony Award nomination. It was for Best Leading Actress in a Musical. The day the nominations were coming out, I knew that if the phone didn't ring by a particular time, I wouldn't have the nomination. I didn't want to sit by the phone waiting, so I went out to do my laundry. When I returned, I opened the door and I knew that if I saw the answering machine blinking, there would be a chance for a nomination. Well, I came in and sure enough there was a message. I was very happy! I was able to enjoy the Tony Ball and all of the pre-Tony events. I bought tickets for my parents, bought my younger brother a tuxedo and told him he would be my escort to the Tonys. My family had been so supportive of me throughout the years that I wanted to share it with them.

A low point for me is when the work is not there. You go through ups and downs in this business. I remember one year it was very slow in New York. It's hard, but you just have to keep believing in yourself and believe that your time will come. Trust in your own talent. Also, when you're working you should prepare for times when it is slow and not spend all your earnings at once.

I think the ethnicity issue is getting a little bit better, but it's still an issue. It's a fact of life in this business. I remember when I was ten, I auditioned for *The Sound of Music* and I had done *South Pacific* at the same theatre. I was told that everyone had to be blonde and blue-eyed and look like a family. I remember thinking "I have a family and I sing and dance." I couldn't understand it, but my parents explained it to me. That was my introduction to type-casting and ethnic role playing. It's difficult, but it's an added element that any minority actor has to deal with.

When I auditioned for the role of Tuptim in *The King and I*, Richard Rodgers was still alive and he came to my audition. I had eight final auditions and twenty-five total because Mr. Rodgers didn't think I could last eight performances a week. I was still under eighteen at the time. Everyone said they wouldn't even see me unless I was eighteen, so I lied and told them I was. I was so worried about my age that when I came in, the director said "June, how are you?" and I said "Eighteen!" I got the role, though, and became the youngest Tuptim on Broadway. I wanted to prove to everyone that vocally I would be able to live up to the part. So, I never missed a show in three and a half years. It was a very good experience in discipline.

It gives me so much pleasure to share what I've been given. For instance, my voice. I believe our talents are gifts from God, and it's a joy to share them with people, bringing happiness to others. When I see people being moved I know I've entertained them. I've taken them out of their world and transported them into another world for two hours. I think everyone who is an actor should not forget that. It's an important part of what we do and we shouldn't become jaded. It's a gift to entertain, and if you're lucky enough to be doing it, do it wisely. There is an expression I believe: "Those who can, do, and those who do, evoke emotion and response."

WORDS OF ADVICE

- Don't get discouraged.
- If it is in you, keep going because your time will come.
- Keep practicing, keep going to your lessons, keep shining and keep polishing your craft when you're not working.
- When auditioning, call upon the sources that make you feel confident in what you can do. You have been prepared for this audition through your lessons, and this is your time to show off.
- When you're nervous and you're doing a singing audition you can run out of air, your voice can shake, your mouth get dry and you'll find yourself swallowing in places where you never needed to swallow before. The only way to control it is to be mentally prepared for the audition. You have to say to yourself "O.K. I want to show you what I can do. I'm happy to sing for you. I'm happy to read for you. Look at me, here I am!"
- Think of it as climbing a mountain. It's a hard struggle, but once you reach the top, the view is incredible!

Part II

LOS ANGELES

21

Robert Foxworth

Robert is originally from Houston, Texas. He attended
Carnegie Mellon University, and he has been pursuing
acting for forty years. At the Old Globe Theatre in San Diego, Robert has performed in *Below the Belt* and portrayed
Elyot in *Private Lives*. He performed *Macbeth*, and Iago in
Othello at the Guthrie Theatre in Minneapolis. He also de-
lighted audiences in *Candide* at the Roundabout Theatre in
New York, as well as *Cyrano de Bergerac* and *Uncle
Vanya* at the Great Lakes Theatre Festival. He has ap-
peared on Broadway and in Los Angeles in *Love Letters*
(with his late wife Elizabeth Montgomery). Robert has
starred in such television movies as *With Murder in Mind*,
Face to Face, Double Standard, Mrs. Sundance, and
Questor. His feature films include John Frankenheimer's
Prophecy and the acclaimed *The Black Marble*. He also
played Chase Gioberti for six years on *Falcon Crest*, and
has guest starred on *Picket Fences*, a two-part *Star Trek:
Deep Space Nine, Outer Limits*, and *The Lazarus Man*. He
is now doing NBC's *Lateline*. Robert is the recipient of the
Hollywood Dramalogue Critics Award for outstanding
achievement in theatre and the Theatre World Award in
New York.

My mother decided to go back to college, and on the campus of the University of Houston was a children's theatre called The Little Red Schoolhouse. She would drop me there as a babysitting service while she attended classes. They cast me in a play called *The Indian Captive*. I was a very shy, awkward kid and all of my classmates came to see me, and with that experience I felt for the first time that I wasn't invisible anymore. It struck a very powerful chord in me, and I understood something about storytelling. I found out that I existed in a way I wasn't cognizant of before.

I've only had one job other than acting in my adult life. I've been very lucky or very stubborn. I went directly from college to summer stock, to Arena Stage in Washington, to New York. One summer when I was in Washington, I worked for ten days selling magazine subscriptions, until I realized it was a way of ripping off poor people. There have also been long periods of unemployment, but as I said, I've been very lucky.

I would not suggest any job to actors. Don't allow yourself the luxury of a security that precludes you from focusing one hundred percent on being an actor. I suppose I say that because that's what I did. I was afraid of becoming secure in something I didn't want to be doing.

One of my highlights is probably what happened to me as I turned fifty and was told that I should be playing the important roles in the literature of theatre. My training had reached its fruition, my life experience had fed me, and my instrument was tuned. When I began to make this change in my sensibility, it reawakened me. I have gained so much joy and satisfaction out of my work in theatre. I realized that I could be doing the roles I always dreamed about when I was a younger man and wasn't equipped to do either technically, vocally, emotionally, or in terms of life experience.

A low point for me was that for a long time, I felt it was more important to get the kind of jobs in television and film that paid me money but gave me no gratification. It was soul-killing to some degree. I allowed myself to go through a period of placing that over the importance to my soul of doing good work.

I hate to make this confession, but I'm going to. I have gotten about three jobs in my life from an audition. I'm a terrible auditioner. However, there were times in my life when I didn't have to do it. I feel insulted when I have to audition for people who don't even know what they're looking for. I can tell from the material when they're waiting for the actor to walk through the door to tell them how the role should be done. In those cases, it doesn't matter what I do. Consequently, I screw it up.

I did an audition once, many years ago, when I had a big mustache. I went into the audition and read, and one of them said "What do you look like without the mustache?" I knew this question would come up, so, I had brought a little paper bag with me. I opened it, took out a pair of electric barber shears, and said, "Let me plug this in somewhere and I'll show you." They started to tell me that I didn't have to do that, and they were laughing, but I said "No, you want to see what I look like," and I shaved if off right in front of them. Well, I got the part. Unfortunately, by the time they were ready to start shooting, it had been cut down so much that I didn't do it.

When looking for an agent, get involved in Equity-Waiver plays, go to the American Film Institute, USC, UCLA, or in New York, NYU, and try to get into student films. Also, get involved with repertory theatre. It's not so great in Los Angeles, but for actors in New York, agents do go to the Arena Stage in Washington, D.C., Washington Shakespeare, Center Stage in Baltimore, Hartford Stage, and the theatre in Philadelphia. They are great places to learn your craft, ply your trade, do great works, and be seen. Some of the smaller agencies are better for a beginning actor because they pay more attention to you. If you get into one of these big "meat locker" agencies too early and you're not quite there yet, you get lost. They've got hot people they're pushing, and that's where the money is. Most of the bigger agencies are not interested in developing talent anyway because they don't have time for it.

Elizabeth and I used to talk about rejection all the time. The rejection she went through as a young actress was so intense that even as an established star of her own series *Bewitched*, when the director said "Cut," she would say "What did I do?" Early on I did not deal with it very well. I carried a lot of rage around with me because of rejection. I brawled, and was an all-around son of a bitch, which fed the problem. It didn't help the problem. The angrier I got and the more I carried on this behavior, the worse the problem of rejection became. However, I started something in my early teens that helped. I met an old actor working at a theatre in Houston who told me that I should get up every morning, open the window, take deep breaths, look out the window and say: "This is my world. I am the best at what I do. Today things will be great for me." I did that, and I would also write about myself. I would write about my hopes and dreams. So there was a residual core in me, despite the rejections, that gave me a little bounce. You have to be tough enough so the rejection doesn't kill your soul, and yet, you have to be sensitive enough that you can continue doing what it is that makes a good actor.

What keeps me going in acting is the fact that I don't paint, I'm not a poet, I'm not a sculptor, I'm not a playwright, screenwriter, or film maker. I have, over my life, grown to love the creative act of making a character come to life, and finding in that character another life in me. I'm not talking about psychodrama, I'm talking about the awakening force of the creative act. I love it so much that there's nothing else I want to do. I have a love of cracking open the meaning of a playwright's or screenwriter's language.

WORDS OF ADVICE

- When doing Shakespeare, start far ahead of rehearsal time to do your research. Then, when you walk into rehearsal you can let it all go, because you've immersed yourself in it and now you're ready to do the work with the text, other actors, and the director.
- If acting isn't something you feel you can't live without, don't do it.
- Most importantly, have a great sense of humor, because you're going to need it!

22

Jaz Davison

Jaz is thirty-eight, originally from Los Angeles, and has been pursuing acting for nineteen years (with a nine-year break to raise her daughter). She received a B.A. in Theatre Arts from California State University, Northridge. Her theatre credits include *Round and Round the Garden* (which she also directed), *Daddy's Dyin' Who's Got the Will?*, *Lost In Yonkers*, *Can-Can*, *Lend Me a Tenor*, *Alice in Wonderland*, *Musical Comedy Murders of 1940*, *Jesus Christ Superstar*, *Pimpernel!*, *Cabaret*, and *The Lion in Winter*.

I decided to become an actor when I was eight years old. I saw *My Fair Lady*, the movie version, and I already owned the Broadway soundtrack so I knew the lyrics by heart. When the overture started I began singing along with it, and my dad leaned over, looked at me, and said "You better stop it or we're going to have to put you on the stage" and I stood up to go! Also, my uncle was a soundman at Twentieth Century Fox studios, and every year for my birthday he would take me to tour the lot until I was eighteen.

I made ends meet by teaching. After my divorce, I went back to live with my dad, got my credential for teaching, and taught at my old high school. I also did make-up for the school plays and wrote a couple of shows that they performed. Even though I wasn't necessarily out there doing my own career, I kept involved. Until I could get someone to watch my daughter, I knew I couldn't just run out and do my acting. So when I got remarried, I was able to get out there.

A highlight for me was when they produced a one-act play of mine at Cal State Northridge called *Losses of the Mind*. One night they had two people signing because it was a special performance for the deaf. I suddenly felt so official! Another highlight was after a performance of mine when I heard a fellow actor say to her friend, "Jaz is the freest actor I've ever met." That meant a lot to me.

A low point was doing work with a theatre group who turned out to be nothing but a bunch of Hollywood "wanna be's," and it was a nightmare. Everyone's ego was in front of the work. At the same time, it was also one of the best learning experiences I ever had!

I prepare for an audition by trying not to laugh! Some of the copy I've been reading for commercial auditions is so ridiculous. I think auditioning is looking at what you can find in the text and making it your own. The best auditions I have are when I just pull out all the stops and have fun. I find one thing I can grab on to, do a great audition, and go back to my seat and fall apart.

I got a good headshot and sent them off to agents. Then a few days later, I took a character that I had written from one of my plays, and she was the one who called the agencies for a follow-up. I was terrified of calling agents and having the phone slammed down on me. So I called up and said "Hi, this is Renee Todd can I speak to (so and so)?" They would say "And what is this regarding?" and I replied, "It's regarding Jaz Davison's performance in *Daddy's Dyin' Who's Got the Will?* We wanted to set up comps." They would have me hold, and sometimes I would get to the agent and sometimes I wouldn't. They were helpful 90 percent of the time. One woman said "Honey, don't call in the morning, we're doing breakdowns. Why don't you call-back later?" Then I would call-back, especially when my baby was asleep, because it sounded more official when I didn't have a one-year-old behind me crying "Mommy!" Luckily, I have a fax machine at home, so the agencies that wanted information faxed to them got it. Also, if they told me they didn't have my information, I would say "I can fax it to you right now." Then I would fax it and sign the cover letter as Renee Todd. When they would ask me who I was (because I couldn't say I was a manager), I didn't know what to say, so I told them "I'm just a good friend who thinks she ought to get a break." Do you know that 90 percent of them said, "Well, good for you!"

I only had one situation where the phone call was better than the meeting. The description of the agency said they handled models but also character actors. So, on the phone I told him that Jaz Davison is a character actress, not a stick. He said that was fine because they handle character actors as well. I went down there and he looked at me like I was dog meat. There were pictures of models all over, and he looked at me like I shouldn't be there. I looked at him and said "I'm Jaz Davison." The look was repeated, until I told him I had an 11:00 appointment with him and Renee Todd set it up. Then he said "Oh yeah, honey, come on in." Suddenly this person, who was *me*, got all this respect! He was still very cold and curt, but he took my picture and told me the owner was gone, but when he got back they would discuss me. I never heard from him again.

When I met with another agent, however, he gave me copy to read, looked at my picture, told me why he didn't like it in a constructive way, and took time with me. He also wanted to see the best ten minutes of my plays on video. When I called him back, he took my call. I also told him that my category is Kathy Bates's little sister, and the ultimate best friend. The minute I said that he said "That's it, Kathy Bates's little sister! I can see that."

Finally, after a commercial showcase night, I called back one of the agencies interested in me, and the woman in the office told me I just had to get my stickers. I didn't know what she was talking about, and she told me it was the stickers with their agency logo to put on my pictures. That's how I found out I was with the agency.

My daughter taught me how to handle rejection. She was signed with an agency and I took her out on some auditions. When she came out I said "How did you do?" She said "Oh, they loved me, let's go." She did get a call-back from that audition, but in the end they decided to cast an older girl. When I told her, she said "What idiots," and I just laughed. I've built the healthiest ego ever. What she really wants to do is to become an animator, so acting is secondary. So I've made it secondary in the fact that, it's what I want to do with my life, but if I don't get a part I'm not going to die. I have two beautiful kids, a marvelous husband, and a dog to come home to. I have a life.

What keeps me going is the adrenaline. It's the enabling factor of becoming somebody else. It's cathartic as well. The last role I did was like being married to a member of my family in which I experienced some abuse, and the role was about a woman who sustained verbal abuse from her husband. It was cathartic because I got to spit on the guy and say "I'm leaving you." I was able to vent, but essentially, I'm crazy! You have to be a little crazy to do acting.

WORDS OF ADVICE

- Don't be afraid to call agencies; just do it.
- Don't wait for the phone to ring. Find or create projects to get your energies out there. Get involved.
- Read plays. If you can, join the Fireside Theatre book club.
- If you aren't certain of who you are and you can't develop something, an agent isn't going to do it for you. You have to come up with a hook for yourself. If you give an agent a hook, they can see dollar signs, and then they know they're going to make money off you.

23

Mary Dryden

Mary was born in Chicago, but was raised in Britain and France and has dual nationality. She has been pursuing acting for thirteen years, after a career as a dancer and model. She received a degree in Elizabethan literature and graduated from the London Academy of Music and Dramatic Art (LAMDA). She has performed in numerous theatrical productions specializing in British roles in the United States, many of them from Shakespeare and Agatha Christie works. Mary has appeared in many student and industrial films, music videos, and commercials. Her feature films include *Private Collections*, *A Situation*, and *The Nutty Professor*.

My parents always said I was a natural performer, and I was always acting for them, putting on little plays. As a tiny girl, I leaped off an entire flight of steps after chirping "Bye, bye!" to my horrified mother. I landed on my feet and made a deep curtsey. I couldn't *not* act.

I had a performing background from ballet and fashion modeling for twenty years and I liked it. I felt like my life was divided into two parts: the literary portion with my degree in Elizabethan literature, and the performing. When I split from my husband, I looked at my life as if it were an apple that had been split into two parts and the only thing that bridged them was acting. It included the literary and the performing. At the time, I was in Los Angeles and I didn't know anybody. I thought "If I fall on my face, no one will notice." I felt that I had nothing to lose. So it was through a personal crisis that I came to acting.

I also had recurring dreams about being on stage. One was really quite comical. I dreamed that I was in a Shakespearean, Roman play. I was wearing a striped dress on one shoulder, standing around columns with men wearing togas. It was a nightmare, though, because I forgot my lines! I hated that dream, and I had it several times. The only thing that made me feel all right about it was knowing that I would never be an actress so it would never happen, and then it did. I was playing Portia in *Julius Caesar* outdoors at the Page Museum. Because it was outdoors anyone could come right up to us. There was a wino who in the middle of my monologue came up and threw mushrooms at me. I was so startled that I forgot my lines, and I thought "Oh, my god, this is it. This is the dream!" Even the actor playing Brutus was no help, he was startled as well. I whispered to him "Help me!" and he whispered back, "I can't!" In the end I was grateful because it was over with and it would never happen again. Now I don't have a problem with lines.

If I need a week off to shoot a commercial in Seattle, I can use vacation and sick time. If you can possibly work part-time and get away with it, that's the best—if you can afford to live on what you make part-time. Being a waiter in the evenings also will free your days for auditions. I have never been very good at that type of work, however.

There's a highlight at every bend in the road; and if there weren't, there wouldn't be much point in going on. If things didn't keep getting better, it wouldn't be fun, interesting, or encouraging. A turning point for me was being cast by Michael Codron in *Anthony and Cleopatra* in London, when I was just coming out of LAMDA. Another highlight was performing *Come and Go* by Samuel Beckett with only three women, in almost total darkness. There was so much space between the lines (in Beckett fashion) that we literally had to count to ourselves to get the timing right. It was like doing a ballet underwater in the dark. It was as though I were floating on a wonderful voyage and I didn't know where I was going, but it felt fantastic. I also got some of the best reviews in my life, but Beckett is such a hard sell in Los Angeles that we had to close early because no one was coming.

One of the low points in my career was having to do a nude love scene for a film. That was without question the hardest thing I had to do in my entire life and I have no intention of ever doing it again. They kept asking me back even after I said I wouldn't do a nude scene. We danced around it for three weeks, and the word they finally used was "glimpses." I believed them, and the very important lesson I learned is that no one protects the actress, the actress has to protect herself. If you don't want a piece of film to be shot, don't allow it to be shot. If you *are* going to have a nude love scene, make sure you have some control and make friends with the director of photography so that he's on your side.

I can't tell you how many auditions I have been to where women will come up to me, reading for the same role as I am, and say "Have you read the play? What's it about?" I can't imagine anything more stupid than not knowing the context of your character. So whenever possible, read the entire play before you audition, not just your character. If it's a film and you only have sides, then read as much as you can. If you have extra time beforehand, read some sides that aren't for your character so you can see what else is going on. The context is very important. Also, don't move much because it affects your voice. If it isn't possible to memorize the scene before going in, memorize the first line and the last line. You also have to react to the other actor when you're not speaking. Even if you're working with another actor with whom you don't get along or who isn't very talented, you can still look good if you're paying attention and listening to the other character.

I got my agent from doing a play in Los Angeles. Being married to a photographer, I never had any problem getting nice photographs. I had a particularly nice photo that I sent out with a cover letter on really fine paper. When they got the envelope the letter was on top, but they could see through it and see my face underneath. I sent it out the opening week of the play and said I was a London-trained actress who was seeking representation and would be happy to comp anyone who wanted to see the play. Well, no one came to see the play, but I had seven calls from agents who wanted to interview me. From those seven interviews, I chose an agent whom I'm still with on the basis of how I felt about him. He wasn't a big agent at the time although he has gotten bigger since, but I felt I wanted someone who understood me, who I feel comfortable with, and who wasn't going to make me do roles I didn't want to do. He also had to understand that I'm not the average nineteen-year-old, blonde-haired, blue-eyed kid from Malibu. I'm a sophisticated actress who's European in nature as well as in appearance. They've got to know what the goods are. Get an excellent photograph, spend as much money as you can afford, and be smart about the photograph. Make sure it's high-contrast and uncluttered. That is, uncluttered background, uncluttered clothing, and if you're a woman, uncluttered hair, make-up, and jewelry. Make it as simple as possible, and as arresting as possible in terms of black and white. It helps to be performing in a play and to offer to comp an agent when you send out the photo.

Rejection is not hard. You've got to realize that it's not you up there, it's someone else. You are being someone else. After working in Britain and America, I've found that particularly in Hollywood, women (especially) are judged and selected more on the basis of their appearance than their talent. I don't necessarily mean whether you're pretty or not, or whether you have a nice figure. I mean that if they want a blonde, they are only going to choose a blonde. So a lot of it just boils down to something that you have no control over and you just have to go with it. The actor is not in charge of the selection process, so you have to turn it over and understand that it's their prerogative to choose whomever they want. My attitude is this: even if they don't want me, they've seen me. I've had people hang on to my picture for years and call me later for a role. It's happened twice.

Acting is a special place, it's what keeps me going. I treasure a quote from Gabriel Byrne's book *Pictures in My Head* in which he says, "We embrace acting without question again and again whether it brings us joy or not, for there is always the belief, buried deep, that we unlock the doors with a golden key to a time and a place that is beyond dreams, beyond imagination, somewhere between the shadow and the substance."[1] You're not you, you're not a fictional character, but you're somewhere in between, and that is very real. It moves people to tears and to laughter and has done so for centuries. It's been one of the most consistently important parts of civilization since civilization existed. Theatre is terribly important to understanding the human condition and to be a part of that is a privilege.

WORDS OF ADVICE

- Read a lot of plays and literature. It's helpful to know something about history and literature for certain periods.
- Read aloud every day for fifteen minutes.

- Cultivate your voice. Learn how to speak clearly, find your natural voice register, and learn to project even when you're whispering. Learn to do dialects and, if you can, learn languages.
- For women, if you find your voice is going into a higher register, take off your shoes (especially if they're high heels), take a deep breath, and your voice will be back to where it should be.
- Leave your ego at the door. Acting is not about ego.

NOTE

1. Gabriel Byrne, *Pictures in My Head* (Niwot, CO: Roberts Rinehart, 1995), p. 70.

24

Jonathan Coogan

Jonathan is thirty-six, originally from Los Angeles, and has been pursuing acting for ten years. He studied at the Lee Strasberg Theatre Institute and the Tracy Roberts Actor's Studio. Jonathan's theatre credits include *Lost in Yonkers*, *Sweet Charity*, *Sister Mary Ignatuis Explains It All For You*, *Barefoot in the Park*, *The Odd Couple* (female version), *Death of a Salesman*, *Wait until Dark*, *The Crucible*, *Private Wars*, and *Fatal Attraction*. His television credits include *Married . . . with Children*, *Uncle Buck*, *Mimi and Me*, *Top of the Heap*, and *Life's Work*. He has also appeared in commercials and co-starred in the independent film *The Dress*.

I decided to become an actor after getting tired of just waking up every morning and going to work. All my life I had heard, "You should try acting, you've got a great voice, and you're funny," but because of my family history, my mother wanted me to stay away from it. Jackie Coogan was my uncle, who played opposite Charlie Chaplin in *The Kid*. My father, Robert Coogan, was also a child actor like my uncle, but my grandmother lost my uncle to the world because he was so famous after being in *The Kid*. So my father became protected by my grandmother and she spent the money that Jackie made on him. This created the

Coogan Law, which is now the child labor law. So, because of all the problems associated with the limelight, my mother wanted to keep me as far away from it as possible. I just never got into it and she never pushed me into it.

I was in an accident, and during rehabilitation I realized didn't want to go back to my job. So I went to the Lee Strasberg Theatre Institute, paid $5,000 and went full time to acting school. I decided if I was going to do this, I didn't want to embarrass myself and I took it very seriously. I wanted to give acting a chance or else I would look back and hate myself for not trying.

My stepfather retired and I took over his scrap metal company. It's a one-man operation; I've got a truck and some accounts, and it pays the bills. It also allows me the freedom to go on interviews and auditions. My customers are all aware of my aspirations in acting and they ask me when I'm going to be on television again or in a play. It's good for me and it's good for my business, because they see that I'm someone else besides just some guy who stops by once a week to pick up their scrap.

Like the billboard says on Sunset Boulevard "You're an actor, what restaurant?" Being a waiter brings instant money in tips, which keeps cash in your pocket, and there's flexibility. Whatever business you're in, make flexibility a necessity. I sold cars for ten months and one day I had to go to an audition during work hours and my bosses were not sympathetic. They told me I had to immerse myself in their business and be a car salesman. I said "I don't want to be a car salesman until I die. I'm sorry." They fired me and I thanked them. I collected unemployment and went back to work for my stepfather. Find something you enjoy being around. It may not sound easy, but you will build resentment with the people you work with and with yourself if you hate your job. If you start hating yourself, then you can't be 100% when you go on auditions. You have to be in a good space.

A highlight for me was when I decided to get into the professional acting world. My friend's cousin was a casting director working on *Married . . . with Children.* He called her and said "I want you to get Jonathan an audition." When I walked into her office, she said she had a part I could read for. She had me read, gave me a little direction, and asked if I would read the next day. I came in the next day and read for the producers, writers, director, and assistant director. I was to audition after a dozen other actors, some of whom I recognized from other television shows, and who all looked just as blue-collar as I did. I thought to myself, "Well, I never had a job acting professionally, so I won't expect anything." Since I had that attitude, I went in with no expectations, and I was natural. When I was finished, they said "That's it." I said, "That's it? O.K. I'll see you guys on the set." I was that casual about it because I didn't know how to react. I went into the hallway to use the pay phone. I was waiting in line for the pay phone and the casting director came out and nodded her head at me. I said "Don't nod your head at me like that unless I've got the job." She said, "You got it" and I broke down crying. I couldn't believe it!

A low point for me was when I co-starred on the television show *Uncle Buck*. The episode was in the *TV Guide*, but since it had low ratings, they aired the show they filmed after mine because it guest starred Kareem Abdul-Jabbar. The following week Desert Storm started so the show was pre-empted, and after that it was canceled. That was such a disappointment because of all the work I had put in previous to that show.

When you're auditioning, you'll find that many times they will give you different lines when you arrive and you can't let that throw you. In that case, just tell them you need five or ten minutes to look the lines over. I did that once and was told I couldn't take the time because they were going to be gone in five minutes, so I said "Well, I don't usually work well under pressure, but can you allow me to take a few deep breaths?" and I got a laugh out of them. Then I was comfortable. You have to be comfortable in your audition situation and you have to take care of yourself. Most likely they'll respect you for that. Don't give your best audition in the car on the way home, give them the best you've got. The biggest lesson I've learned from losing jobs is that you have to go into an audition and do the best you can with no expectations.

I got my agent because I asked a friend of mine who was in the business and was on a television show to send his agent down to see me in a play. I said, "I want you to bring your agent down so he can tell me I stink and I should get out of the business, or that I'm wonderful and I need to take more classes. I need some professional feedback." There's a lot of fear involved in that because you never know what to expect. After he saw me, he had me come in and meet someone else at the agency. They asked me to read for them and just after that, I got the job on *Married . . . with Children*, so the following week I signed a contract.

If you take rejection personally, you're going to drive yourself nuts and end up running away from the business. When my agent left the agency and new agents came in, they still sent me out on auditions because I was doing another play and they could see I was active. When those agents left and new agents came in again, I got frustrated. Then I got a call from the agency and they said, "We just came across your demo tape and we were wondering, did you want to pick it up or should we recycle the tape?" At this point I realized I didn't have representation anymore and they had dropped me as a client. That's how they said it. My professional work wasn't worth keeping is how I took it, and that was major rejection for me. I put acting on the back burner and was very disenchanted with Hollywood and agents. I just backed off. I didn't do any acting again for about a year. I didn't want to send pictures out to twenty agencies and have nobody call me. I was living in the fear of rejection. I was assuming I was going to be rejected so I wouldn't do the footwork. What I had to learn was that this is a business where I have to take chances, and I had to learn how to accept rejection. Now I'm taking improv classes and actor's seminars. I'm ready to submit my pictures again.

What keeps me going is my love for acting and even the rehearsal process—the creation of a character, the learning of the play and of the part. Sometimes I don't get paid a penny and I have to help build the set, but that doesn't bother me at all, it makes me feel more a part of it all. It's the creativity of acting that keeps me wanting to do more and draws me back to the theatre time and time again.

WORDS OF ADVICE

- Do a lot of theatre. The majority of casting directors and people I've met in the business are impressed by the amount of theatre I've done.
- Show up early to your audition and always be polite.
- Practice makes perfect; go on as many auditions as possible.

25

Kerry Carnahan

Kerry is thirty-two and is a graduate of the University of California, Irvine, with a B.A. in Fine Arts/Dance. She has been pursuing musical theater for seventeen years. Originally from Tokyo, Japan, she has performed in *Oklahoma!*, *Oliver*, *Chicago*, and *Dames at Sea*. She also performed in a regional tour of *Work It!* in New York. She appeared in the Long Beach Civic Light Opera's production of *The Wizard of Oz* with Cathy Rigby, and played Connie Wong in a regional theater production of *A Chorus Line*. Kerry marked her first performance with the East West Players as Gussie in Stephen Sondheim's *Merrily We Roll Along*. She has performed at the Sports Arena, Dodger Stadium, and Santa Anita Park, singing the national anthem.

When I was very young my sister took ballet. One day I went in to watch her and I loved it. I begged my mother to let me take ballet and she agreed. I had to be five years old to be admitted in the academy, so

I started then. When I went to college my major was undeclared. At the end of my sophomore year when I was taking my final in ballet, my teachers invited me to be a dance major. There was nothing else I was passionate about, so I took it.

I work part-time as an administrative assistant in a Japanese corporation. I also worked as a production assistant to a man who interviewed celebrities. When he interviewed Audrey Meadows she said, "Never let a 'day job' get in the way of your acting, and go to every audition." I've always remembered that. I need to work in order to pay bills, but my goal is to make a living solely from performing—whether it be acting, singing, or voice-overs.

I hit a low point six years ago and decided to forget it. I thought "I'm not going to do this any more. It's too hard, it's too painful." I lost vision. I started going to school for interior design. I was losing focus because I let the fact that it was so hard overtake me. I also gained a lot of weight. The people around me were urging me to lose weight, and they wanted the best for me. They supported me but would give me hard talks, and I appreciated that. I read a book about overeating, and I understood that it was my own fear. I worked at getting the weight off. Then I faced the fact that I missed performing, and I always wanted to know if I could make it as a musical theatre performer. I thought, "If I don't do it now, I will never know."

I think ethnicity makes a difference, but I think it's making less of a difference. I'm hoping that the more multicultural the world becomes, the more opportunities there will be for artists of all races to be represented in all art forums. I think there are a lot more Asian people in the theatre now than there ever were. The East West Players was started by a group of Asian American actors because they were tired of doing stereotypical roles. They created a company where Asian actors could perform in roles they would otherwise not have the opportunity to perform in, as well as have a place where Asian writers could showcase original work. In fact, they have done so well that not only are they moving to a larger facility, but they are the foremost Asian theatre in the country, and many of the actors who started out there have gone on to win awards for work on Broadway, television, and film.

I prepare for a musical theatre audition by doing a vocal warm-up from a tape I made earlier with my voice teacher. Doing something physical like running up a flight of stairs gets my breathing going and breathing steam in the shower helps my voice to relax. I also believe that studying with a good voice teacher is so important and has been key in teaching me strength, versatility of style, and vocal technique.

Once I had an audition for *Miss Saigon* and my voice cracked on the high notes. I was in my range, so I was very surprised. That had never happened to me before. The pianist was very nice, dropped an octave down for me, and started again. I was really depressed about it, but I got past it with the help of encouraging friends and my husband. I now realize that vocally I hadn't prepared correctly. At the time, I was performing in a musical, sang every weekend at my church, and also sang in a dinner show on Sunday nights. I had been abusing my voice by pushing without proper placement of my voice. My voice teacher has helped me correct that problem.

People always tell me that I have great potential. I want to see if I can take that potential to its full fruition. I have been riding on natural talent, and not much discipline. Self-discipline has been my weakness, and I have to overcome it. I have to have the integrity to stick with this and make it happen all the way to the end.

WORDS OF ADVICE

- Persevere.
- Don't get down when it seems as if it's not going to happen.
- Stay on top of your training.
- For musical theatre auditions, make sure that you have your shoes and music set out the night before. That way you don't have to worry about it the next day.
- It is very important to be vocalizing daily to build strength, and to be able to command your voice to do whatever you need at the time.
- Stay in contact with the people you meet.
- Keep a support group of friends and family strong around you.
- Don't lose sight of what's important. If you don't get the job, it's not the end of the world.

26

Reena Phillips

Reena Phillips has been pursuing acting for over ten years. Originally from Houston, Texas, she attended the University of Houston, then moved to New York after receiving a dance scholarship at Alvin Ailey for two years. She studied the Meisner technique, attended the Neighborhood Playhouse, and has performed at Radio City Music Hall. Her theatre credits include *Ain't Misbehavin*, *Sophisticated Ladies*, *Dreamgirls*, and *You Can't Take It With You*.

In high school I was always the class clown. I also had an interest in dance, but I never had any formal training. Apparently I had a talent for it because I beat out a lot of other dancers for the Alvin Ailey scholarship. Then I branched out into musical theatre.

I now own my own catering business, and I used to work in telemarketing sales between theatre jobs. I was in good with my supervisor at work; so when I needed a day off to audition, she was cool about it. Some people try to wait until the next acting job, but if you haven't hit it where you are working regularly, you've got to do something in between. Otherwise, when you go into auditions you look and feel desperate. You have to be in it for the love of it, because it's definitely not for profit in the beginning.

I had one bad experience as a waitress because I wasn't that good as a waitress. I worked at a lunch/deli place and the manager didn't like me. Maybe he could see in my attitude that I really didn't care, and that the job wasn't that important to me. He would scream at me a lot and bring me to tears. One day I was near the end of a shift and I had one customer left. I finished with the customer, gave him the check, and at a certain hour I could have dinner myself, so I did. I was sitting there eating my dinner, and the manager came over and screamed "You're not finished with your customer yet, you put that food down." I didn't like the way he screamed at me in front of everyone, so I took my time and ate my food. He went to the waitress schedule and started scratching my name off real hard, flipping the pages. I knew then that he was firing me. So, I went in the back and got my big dance bag. I got a pie plate and filled it with whipped cream about six inches high. He was wearing a blue suit. I walked over to him and pushed the plate of whipped cream right in his face. Whipped cream was dripping down his suit, and everyone in the restaurant started laughing hysterically. He was embarrassed because I did it in front of all the customers. I held my head up high, walked out the door, and never looked back. It was one of the best moments of my life.

One of the highlights of my career was when I performed at Radio City Music Hall as the lead for almost a week. Never in my wildest dreams did I think that after being in New York for two years I would be starring at Radio City.

Since I've been in Los Angeles it has been my lowest point. In New York I lived and breathed what I did, but out here I've gotten caught up in working and paying the car note. I started worrying too much about making money as opposed to just doing what I love to do, but that will end soon because I love acting too much.

Rejection is tough. Especially after you've gone through call-backs, gotten down to the end, and it's between you and one other person. It's depressing, but you have to snap yourself out of it because if you get in that depressive state, it will drive you away from the business. What I do is work out, go to a class, or do something active to release that feeling. I know people who are doing great, but they're always depressed because they haven't gotten that big role they want. I think that's one of the things you have to look out for; its not being enough for you—instead of sitting down and counting your blessings. I've done ten jobs this year. That's a blessing.

I made it to the third call-back for *The Josephine Baker Story*. In preparing, I studied videotapes and documentaries of her. I also had to make up a dance for part of the audition, so I went to a studio and created a dance. I was going to get this job! I went to the third call-back and they videotaped us. I had to do six different scenes on tape, so I hired a coach to work with me, and made my own costume. When I didn't get the part, it took me a while to get over it, because I knew it could have been my big break. What made that role so special was that every time I was on stage, people told me I looked like Josephine Baker. Lynn Whitfield is a great actress, though, and did a wonderful job.

What always keeps me going is that burning itch to be on stage, and that's something that has to be inside. You can't force that, it has to be inside of you.

WORDS OF ADVICE

- Study. Make sure you're good at what you do before you go out there.
- Be prepared. You are going to be competing against serious actors.
- Be confident.
- Study voice and movement. Even if you can't dance, take some basic dance training so you can play different roles and be flexible. If you can sing, you will want to develop and train your voice.
- Find something else to fall back on as well.
- Make sure you really love what you're doing, otherwise you're just wasting your time.

Jack Stauffer

Jack is fifty years old and has been a professional actor for thirty years. Born in New York and raised in Connecticut, he was a member of the original cast of *All My Children*, playing the role of Chuck Tyler. On *Battlestar Galactica* he played the role of Bojay, and he was also a series regular on *The Young and the Restless*. He has starred in two television pilots, appeared in numerous miniseries, movies for television, and guest-starred on 45 television episodes. He has also done over 250 commercials. He performs regularly in numerous theatre venues throughout Southern California, from 110-seat houses all the way to 5,000-seat amphitheaters. His favorite role is Harold Hill in *The Music Man*. Recently he starred as Fagin in *Oliver*, appearing with Adam Wylie of *Picket Fences*, and played opposite *The Phantom of the Opera*'s Dale Kristien in *My Fair Lady*.

I grew up in the industry. I was born into it because both my parents were producers. Now, to supplement income, I coach tennis. If you need a job to make ends meet, get any type of job where you can set your own time and hours. You can't work for a company unless they are very flexible. For actors trying to get an agent, I suggest putting together five minutes of dynamite videotape—whether it's from a musical, a workshop, or a student film—and send it out. Also, do theatre or showcases that agents might see. I'm a firm believer in doing student films as well. You never know who is directing a student film and might be known later on.

The worst decision I ever made was in 1976. I had two offers for the lead role in a series. One was through Columbia and was about a futuristic high-tech mobile medical unit. The other script was from MGM, and to this day it was the worst script I have ever read in my life. It was this god-awful thing about highway patrolmen on motorcycles. So, I accepted the Columbia pilot and I ended up doing one show. The other show became *C.H.I.P.S.* and made Larry Wilcox a millionaire.

When it comes to auditions, use them like a performance. This is the hardest thing to teach actors. I can't tell you how many times I've walked into an audition and somebody says, "Now look, this is just an audition, we don't expect a finished performance. We don't expect you to be polished." That's not true. They expect *Gone with the Wind*, and you better give it to them, because somebody else will. So never go on an audition unprepared. You wouldn't walk out on stage in front of an audience without having rehearsed, so don't go to an audition without having rehearsed. Try to get the script ahead of time. If you only have sides, go down to the audition an hour early, make friends with the secretary, get a copy of the script, and sit in the corner and read it. You will be surprised at how different your line reactions will be according to what happens in the plot.

Actually, if you look up the term Actor, what you should find is: *see* paranoid schizophrenic. Basically, what do you call someone who's ambition in life is to run around and pretend to be somebody else? It's because we won't grow up. When we're children we're blessed with imagination. When I was a boy I would peek around the seawall in front of my house with my toy gun, get shot, and die on the lawn. However, eventually somebody will issue the ultimate challenge: "When are you going to grow up?" That's when you have to make the decision whether or not to truly pursue your craft. A famous director once said, "I do not want an actor who wants the role. Find me the actor who needs the role."

WORDS OF ADVICE

To be a good actor you need:

- Ability. Some people have a flair for drama, some people don't. You need that basic flair.
- Imagination. To be able to be another person, put yourself into another situation, and allow that situation to become real for you.
- Ego. You need to know, beyond a shadow of a doubt, that whatever you do is good.
- Honesty. Be honest in your work. It comes from the truth of the character, the truth in what you say, and the truth of the material. You must be true to what the author intended.
- Vulnerability. Be willing to risk it all. Be able to throw your emotions out in front of the world and have people trample on them.
- Discipline and practice. Be prepared both mentally and physically. You must know precisely why you do or say something, otherwise you won't be able to recreate that event. Being brilliant once is lucky, doing it over and over is being professional.
- Passion. You have to want it more than anything. The industry is totally unforgiving and has no tenure. You'd better be able to accept it, and that takes great inner strength.

28

Vance Valencia

Vance is forty-five years old, originally from Los Angeles, and has been pursuing acting for twenty-one years. He graduated from California State University, Los Angeles, and joined the Nosotros theatre company, one of the oldest Hispanic theatre companies in Los Angeles. Besides working at Nosotros, Vance has done numerous plays, including productions at the Attic Theatre, Los Angeles Actors Theatre, and the Globe Theatre in San Diego. He has appeared in four miniseries, and twenty-five television episodes, including guest-starring roles on *Beverly Hills 90210* and *Profiler*. Vance has also appeared in five films, including featured roles in *Die Hard* and *Contact*. He is currently producing theatre as well as acting.

What turned me on about acting was the sheer fun of getting up and entertaining. Making people laugh, and enjoying the life that's on stage. It's a land of make-believe, and the imaginative child in all of us never dies. It's still as alive and well for me today as it was thirty years ago.

I worked at a school where my title was Technical Director. I designed lights for dance shows and plays, and taught students how to build sets and use lighting. Do something that makes you happy. Don't stay too long in a job that doesn't make you happy. For me, being a substitute teacher was the best job because I picked the days I wanted to work and got off on the days I needed to audition. You don't want to be worried about not getting a job as an actor, *and* about how you're going to pay the rent. You've got to take care of the necessities. That is what's hard about the profession of acting. If you think you can only work as an actor, and that's all you can do (and you're not independently wealthy), you're going to hit hard reality soon.

When you start going to auditions with the attitude that you don't need the job, they want you. Casting directors can sniff out desperation and need, and they will weed you out immediately. It's like that old deodorant commercial says: "Never let them see you sweat." You have to look at yourself as unique and special; and if you don't feel that way, no one else will do it for you. There are other actors who feel that way, and they're going to be fighting just as hard as you. Getting work deals with having work, having a bank account, living comfortably enough to feel good about yourself. Then you exude that kind of confidence you need. They would much rather have the opportunity to hire confident people for the job. Our personal life as actors has a direct flow back and forth from who we are as people. Also, you're still a person before you're an actor, so if someone asks you to do something to get a part that you don't want to do, don't do it.

A highlight for me has been my work on the stage. It's magic to do theatre. Some of the theatres were so small, the audience was close enough to catch the red gel-lighting on my hair. In those instances, I really got an opportunity to show who I was, what I could do, and bring to life all those emotions waiting inside to come out. I look back at the stage with joy, but my highlight is still coming.

You will be turned down far more times than you will be accepted. You will hear "no" so many times that you may begin to doubt yourself, but these are the things that must happen in order to get to the next level. To thicken your skin, you can't care how many "no's" you hear today; you're living for the "yes" you'll hear tomorrow. The low points are: working through rejection, fighting past not feeling accepted, and learning how to read bad reviews about yourself.

I think there is a difference being a Hispanic actor, and at the same time, there isn't a difference. If a part specifically calls for a Hispanic, then we're up for that role. If the part does not call for a Hispanic and there is no gender attached, then the role should be up to any actor, but many times it isn't open to other ethnicities. That is the problem that opens itself to us. Somewhere in the middle is a happy medium. It all comes back to writing. For years the minorities complained about the stereotypes in the business. The stereotypes are there, but sometimes they are accurate. There are also good, positive role models. We are asking for more jobs to be made available by looking at smaller roles being cast nontraditionally and writing roles that are more positive. If you really want it to be done, don't wait for someone else to write it, because who can write better about their experience than someone who's lived the experience? I was told once auditioning for *St. Elsewhere* that I didn't look like an East Coast Hispanic. They said my hair didn't look Puerto Rican. By saying that, they are determining and perpetuating certain images of Hispanics. After years of this, it has an effect on people. Those are the kinds of issues I look at regarding ethnicity. It can work for me or against me. I deserve the right to play the roles that are worth playing. When I played Brutus at the Globe Theatre in *Julius Caesar*, I didn't hear anyone say "That Mexican can't be Brutus." I'm an actor and that is the bottom line.

What keeps me going is knowing that I haven't peaked. Knowing that I haven't done the ultimate role, knowing that there's more I can do. I'm hungry for it. I'm never finished. That's the beauty of it, knowing that there's no end. There's always another play, another role. I'm always seeking the next level. That's what drives me. It's the hunt that keeps me alive.

WORDS OF ADVICE

- Don't worry about getting typecast, just get cast. Log in the hours, learn how to work, and work!
- You never know who's in the audience, you never know what you're going to gain by doing a show, and each one (even though you may not be getting paid for it) is a job.
- Learn to be a craftsman at acting. Being a craftsman is knowing how to recreate and reinvest all of those emotions that brought you to performance level, and do it again the next night. As it applies to movies and television, it's the ability to recreate those emotions from take to take.
- The best training I think any actor can have is the training of getting up and doing. I think you can spend a lot of time in class, read, and watch movies, but the way to learn to act is to actively pursue it. The more you do, the more you become acquainted with the process.
- Approach every rehearsal as if it were a performance. Don't hold back.

- Keep looking for projects to do. Don't stop at any one thing, be open to all sorts of alternatives.
- When you're ready you will know it. Seek everything out in its own time.
- This is a business also, so you have to come to grips with two things: You are a good actor, but don't rely just on your talent to make it. Focus also on self-marketing factors that come into play, and learn how to work with them.
- Get involved in a theatre company.
- Read a new play every week. Get the trade papers and be aware of what's going on.
- Be single-minded about what matters more to you than anything else, and chase it like the devil's chasing you! Then you're bound to have some success.

29

Whitney Weston

Whitney is originally from Chicago and has been pursuing acting for thirteen years. She received her theatre degree from Columbia College in Chicago. She studied with John Ruskin at the Neighborhood Playhouse in New York, and Stephanie Feury and Playhouse West in Los Angeles. Her theatre credits include *The Sign in Sidney Brustein's Window*, *Cat on a Hot Tin Roof*, *The Butterfly Effect*, *Lend Me a Tenor*, *Porch*, *Last Summer at Bluefish Cove*, *I Ought to Be in Pictures*, and *The Star-Spangled Girl*. Whitney's television credits include lead and co-starring roles in *Instant Recall* (pilot), *Heroes of Desert Storm* (ABC movie of the week), *From the Dead of Night* (NBC miniseries), *Friends*, *The Hollywood Family*, *Up All Night*, and *Under the Biltmore Clock*. She has also appeared in industrial films, commercials, and a slew of independent feature films. Whitney is the founder of New Attitude Productions, a nonprofit 99-seat theatre company.

When I was a kid I used to set up little shows on Saturday afternoons. I would rehearse all day with my friends, then at 4:00 it would be curtain time. Our audience consisted of my parents and usually a neighbor.

Because I started modeling at the age of sixteen, the thought of doing anything theatrical scared me because I had no idea what I was doing. Once I started focusing on theatre, I was able to overcome a lot of the fear just by practice.

I have a couple of my own businesses to keep me going. I work for different caterers. I sometimes manage parties for them and do their displays. That has led to other jobs, especially during the holidays when people need windows dressed. One year all I did was Christmas trees. When you walk into a bank and see a Christmas tree, it doesn't arrive decorated; they hire decorating companies. I was able to do that freelance. It works out well because within the entertainment industry the busy times are spring and fall, and for catering, it's winter and summer. So I can work hard throughout the holidays and then pull out and do whatever I need to do in the spring.

Definitely start your own business. When I do display work, it's fun for me and it's a creative outlet. I get boxes and boxes of stuff and I get to make something. Just to find something other than acting that you enjoy doing will help. I know a lot of actors that have done very well cultivating other talents. For instance, if you're also a bookkeeper, you could approach a theatre company and offer to do their books for a certain amount of money, as well as get into some of their shows. Start a barter system.

A highlight for me was the first time I saw myself on national television. I did a movie of the week with Lindsay Wagner. The only thing that bothered me was I thought my face looked fat. I played an evil character so the camera was pointing up at my face and I was in dark clothes. It was a thrill, but then I had a whole new set of problems when I thought, "This is not what I wanted to look like."

A low point was after I got my first movie in Los Angeles. At the time I was waiting tables. I found out I got the part on a Wednesday and I had to leave on Monday to shoot. On my very last shift, I stood up on a table and announced to the restaurant that this was the last cup of coffee I was going to pour. I poured it, tore off my apron, and the whole restaurant clapped. I thought "Yes! I've arrived." I shot the film and it was great. I came back with all this money and it was gone in two months. I expected it to keep going and it didn't. I got very broke. I realized that it's not just one job that makes you all of a sudden a successful actor. You could go up, you could go down, or you could be in between. That's when I got a day job for a while. It started getting hard because I was going out on commercial auditions almost every day and I hardly ever got called back because I was so stressed about asking for a different lunch hour every day. I would blow the audition because it made me feel so bad that these people were waiting for me back at the office. By the end of my employment I gained fifteen pounds, none of my clothes fit me, and I started dragging myself to work with no make-up. Then the office politics and gossip kicked in and I thought, "O.K., Whitney, somehow you have to get out and find something else."

When I audition, I always memorize the lines before I make any decisions about the character so that I have it line for line. Then I'll work on the character and have it down solid as if I were doing it. They can love it or hate it, but at least I come in with something solid. As far as relaxing is concerned, I've been a Buddhist for twelve years so I'm heavily into meditation, and that helps me to remain focused.

I went to an audition which was for a union industrial film, and since it was union, I thought it would be O.K. When I got to the audition a man told me that to begin with, I would play an amoeba. To do this, they needed to wrap my (nude) body in cellophane, but nothing would show. He asked me if this was O.K. I thought it was bizarre, but I said "I guess." Then he said, "we have to make sure that you're comfortable enough to be wrapped in the cellophane, so would you mind taking off your clothes and standing in my office naked." At that point I left, and when I walked out there was a room full of women waiting to go in. The scary thing about that situation was that if that man had the audacity to ask that question, he was expecting someone to do it. I called SAG later and they had never heard of him.

I produced my first play because I had a hard time getting into a play. All my credits were from college theatre. Nobody wanted to let me in. I understudied a few parts and then got to perform, so I watched how they produced and thought, "Why can't I do that?" I produced my own show and it was a nightmare, but I knew there had to be a way to change it and make it better. That's how I started my theatre company. What I did was to connect all my shows with a charity, which solved a lot of problems. It had a lot to do with egos and with actors wanting to just showcase themselves. When it's tied in with a benefit, and it's not so much about you, but about helping somebody else, the whole atmosphere changes. It's also about actors giving back. Whatever level you're at, you can always give back. There's a sense of pride and camaraderie, and it's a much easier road.

What keeps me going is the fact that I can't imagine doing anything else. I've set my goal. I can't imagine going in any other direction. They'll eventually let me in. It's been getting better over the years because people are starting to know me and my work. I keep popping up over and over again. My auditions are different from when I first came out to Los Angeles, because at first I was new, I was green, and I got little interest. Now, they know that I've been around a while and each time they see me, my resume has more experience on it. Every person I've ever talked to that's successful in the business has said, "If you hang around long enough and do good work, they will eventually let you in." At that point they have to. You're in their face all the time.

WORDS OF ADVICE

- Enjoy the road. Enjoy your way up.
- You're able to do a job that you love, so do it and love it. Someone will eventually hire you for something bigger; but in the meantime, how many people get to do a job that they love?

30

Kristen Miller

Kristen is nineteen years old. She has been acting for eight years, and pursuing it as a career for two. Growing up in Manhattan Beach, her acting debut was at age eleven, playing Laurie in *Brighton Beach Memoirs*. Later, she performed in *The Little Foxes*, *Can-Can*, *Cabaret*, *Working*, and *Guys and Dolls*. She had a supporting role in *Oswego*, which is a new project by *Man of La Mancha*'s lyricist Joe Darion. In college, she portrayed Mallory/Avril in *City of Angels* and also performed in the Young Playwrights' Festival at the Blank Theatre Company. Kristen has appeared in many commercials, guest-starred on *Saved by the Bell*, and had a recurring role on Aaron Spelling's *Malibu Shores*. She played a small role in the film *Dogwatch*, with Sam Elliot and Paul Sorvino. Kristen is currently Ashley Elliot on *USA High*, which airs domestically on the USA Network.

When I was little and played with my friends, I would get the whole block together, set up the video camera in the backyard, and make movies and soap operas. I love watching film and theatre, and watching it makes me want to do it. As an actor, I never get bored. Every day is different, and I'm always working on different things and learning more.

While doing *Cabaret* in community theatre, my choreographer introduced me to a casting agent for commercials, who recommended me to a commercial agent. For a year, I made the rounds of auditions for commercials and filmed a number of them. I was able to work the audition times around the class schedule for my first year of college. Then, my boyfriend's father referred me to a theatrical casting agent who recommended me to a management company. I signed with them. They began sending me to auditions for television and movie roles, and they had me interview with casting directors and theatrical agencies. I put my college studies on hold. Just as I began to get guest roles in television, I signed with my theatrical agents, and the number of my auditions and the quality of the roles increased until *USA High* went into production in July 1996.

I think of auditioning as my regular job, and of my acting job as my reward. Auditioning can be a very hard job; but the more I do it, the more comfortable I get doing it. The acting roles I've had, and particularly my steady work on a series now, are definitely more like a reward than a job.

Commercial auditions were great training for me. There were many of them, and I had little chance of landing any given one. I would make mistakes—lots at first—but I learned not to beat myself up. I just began to think about the next audition.

Now, I feel like I'm ready for almost anything to happen to me at an audition. I've had to learn how to sit in a waiting room for hours and then jump my energy up to performance level on demand. I laugh about being treated like a piece of meat. I've gotten over the surprise of casting directors taking phone calls while I'm in the middle of an emotional scene they're reading with me. I've been told to do an improvisation with another actor, only to have that actor stand absolutely mute (and I got the commercial). I've been given a lengthy script outside an audition, told the words would be shown on a monitor, and then gone inside to tape, only to be told the monitor is not being used, and I'm to do the scene from memory, now! I've been given the wrong sides outside the audition, and been told to dress in a certain way, only to arrive and find everybody else dressed very differently. I've read romantic scenes in which I have to be "in the moment" and convey my character's passion for a boy while the boy's part is being read by a female casting director. I've done lots of readings either where I'm clearly wrong for the part, or where I don't have enough professional credits on my resume yet to justify auditioning for such an important part, but where I'm just trying to show the casting director what I can do so I'll be thought of for future roles. My calls for *Malibu Shores* and *USA High* both came from people having seen me audition for other roles.

I actually like some things about auditions (although I like working a lot more). I enjoy the challenge, having to create a character quickly and from limited information, doing it, and then leaving it behind to go on to the next one. It can be work to keep the energy level up from one audition to the next, when month after month I get rejected more often than I get hired. My parents and friends help by encouraging me. The other actors at auditions help as well. Over time, I see the same people and we are almost all friendly. We seldom feel like we are competing with each other.

Continuing my training, and doing roles in theatre also renews my energy. I work with eleven other actors and my acting coach in a group class. It's hard to let go and do group work, but when I see what we can produce at the end of a long session and over a season, it's inspiring.

WORDS OF ADVICE

- Get good pictures.
- Take your pictures to a trusted teacher and ask that person which picture you should make into your headshot.
- Take an acting class that has been recommended.
- Talk to people with agents, and ask them how they like their agent. Perhaps someone you know and trust could talk to an agent for you.
- Get a good agent. If you don't have a good agent, you won't be progressing forward.
- When you arrive at an audition ready to go and then have to sit for an hour, keep your energy up and stay positive.

31

Jeff Asch

Jeff is twenty-nine, originally from Scranton, Pennsylvania, and has been pursuing acting professionally for six years. He trained at the American Academy of Dramatic Arts in Pasadena and has studied with Joan Darling. His theatre credits include *Broadway Bound*, *Charley's Aunt*, *Legends*, *Hello, Dolly!*, *Cabaret*, *Fiorello*, *Once Upon a Mattress*, *A Midsummer Night's Dream*, and *Guys and Dolls*, and he has performed with the Bilingual Foundation of the Arts in Los Angeles. His television appearances include *Family Matters*, *Step by Step*, a recurring role on *Saved by the Bell*, and a guest starring role on *The Magnificent Seven*. Jeff's film credits include *Adventures in Dinosaur City* for Disney, *Hollywood Cabaret* with Imogene Coca, and *Snitch* with Marlee Matlin. He also performed the role of Barney Rubble in the musical stage show of *The Flintstones* at Universal Studios and can be seen in a national Snickers commercial.

Ever since I was fourteen I knew I wanted to be an actor. I knew automatically that acting was what I wanted to do. Watching movies is what made me want to act.

I consider myself very lucky because I am making my living at acting. I have been making my living consistently with various television shows, commercials, films, and stage productions. I also was paid for performing Barney Rubble in *The Flintstones* at Universal Studios. I never knew how much work I was going to get, though, because there were three different casts for that show which rotated. I have also saved money since high school and that helped immensely. It let me concentrate on auditions rather than a full-time job.

The job I would recommend—which is a horrible, ugly job—is telemarketing. It is very flexible. I couldn't do it for more than four hours a day, but that's all I needed. Just don't get into any job that you have to think about when you come home at night. You want to forget it as soon as you walk out the door.

A highlight for me was when I got the role on *Saved by the Bell*. It was a total surprise. As soon as I got out of school I found out about an audition for a role I was perfect for at Raleigh Studios, where they used to shoot *Saved by the Bell*. So, I went down to audition. I didn't have an appointment or an agent, so I made up a story when I came in and told the receptionist that my agent told me to come down. He looked at the list and told me my name wasn't there, so I said "You're kidding. My agent always screws up!" I knew I was going out on a limb, but this was my role. Just then, the assistant casting director walked by and saw me. She asked me if I had an appointment and I told her "No." She looked surprised and gave me the sides. Then she told me to come back in an hour because everyone was at lunch. That's how new I was to this business, I didn't even know I had arrived at lunch. Lunch is at 2:00 in the afternoon for the entire industry, everyone knows that; but I was so green I didn't. So I came back and read for her, she loved me, and brought me in to read for the head casting director that minute. She then had me read for two other projects she was casting and called me back for *Saved by the Bell*. I came back in a few days and read for the producers, who were very stone faced. The next thing I know, I got a call the same day that I booked the job from my new agent. A friend of mine took me in to see his agent before I got the call-back audition, and she took me on. So I got an agent from getting the job.

A low point for me was all those days I was working telemarketing. Nothing was happening, I couldn't get an audition to save my life. I was doing part-time jobs for two years and making ends meet, but I had no creative reward. I may as well not be alive if I'm not able to be creative. That's what I do! It's the only thing I can do, and I do it well.

That's what also keeps me going, though, and why I will never quit this business, because of the creativity.

Usually when I audition I'm very nervous, even though I've had a lot of auditions, but I channel the nervous energy into the character. It works very well for me. A lot of people can't do that and it works opposite for them, they get nervous and can't say the lines. I can usually identify with the character and the words in the script as soon as I get the sides because I'm such a specific type. I can tell right off the bat if the role is right for me. Then it's easy, I just go in and do the job. I work very simply—the simpler the better. People like to see that. A casting director recently gave me a compliment by telling me how simple my comedy was. She said a lot of actors come in and play everything big, over the top, and they don't play it real.

Rejection was tough in the beginning. As I got older, it got easier. The fewer auditions you have, though, the harder it is to handle. When you don't have as many auditions, you hang on every one. That's how it is for me sometimes because I'm such a type, and I don't get as many auditions as an average six foot, brown-eyed, dark-haired guy would get. I'm a character actor, but I tell myself that the truth is, it's always going to be because of the look. If I don't get a call, I know they went with a different look or style. It's very healthy to remember that, and it's also the truth.

What keeps me going is my love for acting. It is the biggest natural high for me. I could never, ever dream about doing anything else in this world. The fact that it happens to pay so well and it's so in the spotlight are just fringe benefits to me. My love for it is the utmost driving force.

WORDS OF ADVICE

- Keep up your theatre. If you can do theatre you can do anything, and it's a great way to meet people and keep from getting rusty.
- Confidence is of the utmost importance in this business. Once you have that and know you can get work, rejection is no problem.
- You need to save money in order to do what you need to do for acting. Put money aside every week and keep saving.

Joe Greco

Joe is in his sixties, originally from Chicago, and has been pursuing acting for forty years. He studied speech and drama at DePaul University. Joe's theatre credits include *Harvey*, *Tribute*, *You Ought to Be in Pictures*, among many others at the Drury Lane Theatre in Chicago. His film and television credits include *About Last Night*, *Above the Law*, *The Untouchables*, *Only the Lonely*, *The Nutty Professor*, *Jack and Mike*, *Lady Blue*, *Bob* (with Bob Newhart), and recurring roles on *NYPD Blue* and *Beverly Hills 90210*.

As kids, my sister and I used to see movies and when we came home, we acted out the entire film. In high school I was steered away from acting because I wanted to become a professional baseball player, but given the fact that I couldn't hit, bat, or run, I gave that up. I never had that burning desire to pursue acting and go to Los Angeles or New York. I thought, "If it happens fine, it if doesn't, it's no great loss." I just got lucky. When I did my first Equity play I thought, "This is it, now let's get serious" and from that point on I gave it more effort. I very conscientiously applied myself to doing the best I could on the job.

After I graduated from DePaul, I got a straight job at a publishing company as an accounts receivable clerk. I worked there for fifteen years as I was slowly breaking into theatre in Chicago. The general manager was an amateur actor and he loved having actors around the office. He was in his sixties at the time, but he loved the theatre. He would let me come and go whenever I needed. If I was in rehearsal for a play and had to go, he would say, "God bless you! Go knock 'em dead." I would take a week off for rehearsals during the day, and come back to work when we were in performance. Finally, I quit the job to do acting full time and have not had a straight job since, thank God.

What helped get me started in theatre was when a friend put me on the payroll of his theatre building scenery and gathering props, and as soon as he could put me in a show on an Equity contract, he did. One night after a performance, a local Chicago agent encouraged me to come to her office and talk to her, which I did. Then I started doing commercials, voice-overs, and industrial training films. Also, Hollywood discovered Chicago as a place to shoot inexpensively so I started acting in feature films and television.

A highlight for me was a made-for-television movie I did called *The Toughest Man in the World*. I had one of the finer directors around who didn't usually direct that kind of film. Working with him and creating a real "bad guy" character (which I don't get hired to do a lot) was a growing experience. Also, working on *Only the Lonely* with Maureen O'Hara and Anthony Quinn was just a wow!

A low point for me was years ago in Chicago when I went eight months without working. It was one of the slowest periods of work for everybody, and our economy was in a slump. I had in those eight months, maybe four auditions, which was not good. I almost took a straight job again.

I really don't have a set plan for auditions. My goal at an audition is to do the acting job as if I had the job already and we were shooting it. I even say "action" in my head before I start the scene. The casting director looking in my face is my scene partner. That's the only preparation I do and it works for me. If it's a cold reading, I keep my eyes off the page as much as possible. When the casting director is finished with that character's line, I look back at my page, find my line, look at it, look back at the casting director's eyes, and say it as close to the line as I can. It's not perfectly word for word, but I don't care, I'm doing an acting job. They don't want to see me looking at a page and reading. They want to see what I can do.

When looking for an agent, I think mailings work. It's better to mail a headshot with a nice cover letter in something that is more eye-catching than a plain brown envelope. Use something that's different. Why not use a red, white, and blue label on a red envelope? Use something that will force the person to open it. I've also heard people say you can't get past the front door. That's baloney! Go up to the office and see if you *can* get past the front door. If you knock on the door and nobody answers, slip your headshot under the door. I used to go into casting director's offices and say, "Hi, how are you doing?" They would say, "Well, you're not supposed to be here, but hi anyway, Joe!" Don't take it as gospel that they don't return your calls either. When I first came out to Los Angeles I used to be on the phone every day until they would talk to me, and they did. There's a myth that you can't go into their offices. Well, you can! It's a free country! Also, use everybody you know to get to an agent. Ask your fellow actors to take you up to see their agent. If you're the same type, then they probably wont, but if you're in different categories, ask. All they can do it say no. You have to be a little aggressive.

One of the major driving forces for me to pursue acting was my family. I had a family and bills to pay, so I knew I had to get out there and work. My goal now is to get out there, get the jobs, and make some money so we can travel.

WORDS OF ADVICE

- Go to New York City, get a part in a good Off-Broadway show, get some good reviews, and they will come after you.
- Do everything you can. Sooner or later, you will hit it. It may take years, but you will hit it.

Denny Evans

Denny is fifty years old, originally from Kentucky but was
raised in Detroit. He solidly worked as an actor for twenty
years and has been teaching his own acting and comedy
workshop for ten years. He studied for six years with Harvey Lembeck (from the acclaimed *Sergeant Bilko* series) in
his comedy improvisation workshop. Denny has appeared
in forty national commercials and worked as a regular on
the *Peter Marshall Variety Show*. He was under contract
with ABC when NBC bought him to star in his own series,
for which he filmed a pilot. Denny was also nominated for
an Academy Award for a short film he wrote and produced
called *Good Morning*, which ran in theatres for years on a
double bill with Woody Allen's film *Bananas*.

The thing that made me decide to become an actor was laughter. Getting a laugh. Growing up, I watched television all the time. Back then,
the main shows were *I Love Lucy*, *Sergeant Bilko*, and *The Dick Van
Dyke Show*. That's when television was at its best, and I was influ-
enced a great deal by it. Also, at school I was the class clown.

I only did one job besides acting. I was an usher at a movie theatre for three months. It worked out well, because I worked at night and had my days free to audition. Then I started getting national commercials and the residuals kicked in and kept me going. Do anything where it's not a hassle to leave. Be up front with the employer and tell them you're an actor. Try to get an evening job or part-time job, because a full-time job will drain you. I don't care how young you are, it will drain you. Make the sacrifices necessary if you truly want to be a working actor.

A highlight for me was getting an Academy Award nomination at the age of twenty-three. It was just a thrill to rent a tuxedo, escort my wife to the awards, and hear Ann-Margret read off my film as one of the nominees. I didn't win, but being nominated was wonderful. They gave me a nice plaque. Based on that Academy Award nomination, the American Film Institute gave me and my partner a grant to do a second short film, which we did, and that film also played in theatres. After that, I got into television and that has been the bulk of my work.

Do acting for the sake of the work rather than for money. Many times actors will take projects that they really don't want to do because of the money. Even if you don't have a lot of money, it will make you unhappy. I didn't have a low point in my career because I never took something just for money.

Improvisation is a great place to experiment and get the confidence that's needed for an audition. Going to a workshop once a week, getting on stage, thinking on your feet, trying different things, and getting response is more rewarding as a confidence builder than any kind of rehearsal at home alone with the copy. You get a sense of a lack of inhibition. I would suggest that actors have a place to go like that once a week whether they're actively working in the industry or just starting out. As far as preparing at home, the best thing to do is keep that frame of mind of not being intimidated or inhibited. The first couple of auditions I had, I blew because I thought I was going to die if I didn't get the part. I remember holding the copy, reading the role and thinking, "I've got to get this!" Just don't take it so seriously. It's hard to obtain that unless you have a place where you can get up and be free enough to lose all those inhibitions that you have before an audition. It's just another day in your career and it's not the only job, and certainly not the last job that you'll ever be reading for. If you're relaxed, the people who are about to hire you will see that, and then they will relax.

I got an agent from being in the Harvey Lembeck workshop. Harvey brought me down to a commercial reading and told them I would be good for the job. Well, I got the job, and the next morning five different commercial agents called my house and said "Would you like to be represented?" So I chose one. I got the television commercial first, then the agent, but Harvey got me the commercial.

The second time I went on an audition, I was rejected. I realized then that it wasn't as easy as I thought. Look at it as a life-long effort. If you say you're going to give it your life, then you look at auditions and rejection as part of it. After a while the acceptances will balance out the rejections. You have to be able to handle it when they say "You didn't get it."

What keeps me going is the love for acting. I actually love the work itself. My work is comedy, and the laughter is wonderful. The best thing you can do in comedy is to just enjoy it. Don't take it so seriously. That's what Harvey Lembeck taught me, so I feel like he passed the baton to me, and now I'm carrying it forward.

WORDS OF ADVICE

- As soon as you get that usher or waiter job, you are then in the industry because that's part of an acting pursuit.
- Stay away from agents who ask for money up front and say they will make you a star, because that's not an agent, that's a con artist.
- Nothing can happen to you unless you are seen, not just by agents but by audiences as well. If an agent is in the audience, that agent will listen to the audience's response.

34

Gabrielle de Cuir

Gabrielle has been pursuing acting for seventeen years. She was raised in Italy, but completed her training as a cum laude graduate of UCLA's theatre department. Her stage credits include *The Man Who Came to Dinner* at the Glendale Center Theatre, *Two Gentlemen of Verona* at the Globe, and *Can-Can* at the Westchester Playhouse. As a company member of the Knightsbridge Theatre in Pasadena, she played lead roles in *Situation Comedy*, *Spider's Web*, and *Accomplice*. Her television credits include national commercials for Sheraton and Safeway. Her most recent film work includes the leading role in Nancy Wyatt's *Misconception* for the American Film Institute.

I chose acting because I just felt so good doing it once I got over the initial few years of being very, very nervous. In high school I can remember feeling like I wasn't breathing before I went on. Once I got beyond that, I felt it was a magical place to be. Being on the stage is the safest place in the world. Something wonderful happens for me, and hopefully, something wonderful happens for the audience as well.

The type of "day job" you do really depends on who you are. I think it's important that the job be something from which you can get satisfaction. If you're totally miserable, you're going to clam up creatively. For many years I worked for an airline in reservations. The freedom I felt when I cut from the job was so liberating, and the ratio of call-backs I went on increased immensely. Now I am fortunate enough to be working at home editing books for audiocassette. It's wonderful because I can leave the computer if I have an audition, and I work my own hours. I don't believe in the phrase "Have something to fall back on." I hate that phrase. "Fall back on" makes it seem inherent that you're going to fail.

When it comes to rejection, I think I have to some extent developed an ability to let it go. It may hurt at the moment, but I let it flow over me, and then just keep going. There are too many uncontrollable factors in casting. You can't figure it out, and if you try to figure it out, it will drive you nuts.

The only way I feel comfortable and I know an audition is going to be successful is if I'm prepared. If I have a script, by God, I better know that thing. If it's for a commercial and I need to improv, I better know three different ways I'm going to attack it. Now, with those in mind; I let it go. I have been able to make the audition part of the acting process, and the enjoyment I get on stage is the same enjoyment I get in that little casting office for five minutes. I love it. It's a chance to perform. It's taken me a long time to get to that point, but I know now, there's only good that can happen in there.

I have an agent, and when I did my mailing I targeted ten agents I felt would be open to me at that point. I also learned that the agent was not going to make me. They are simply there to get you the opportunity, and book you. They're not there to see your plays, hold your hand, and feed you breakfast in the morning. The Hollywood image that an agent is supposed to make you a star is not reality. Once you realize that, then you can use the situation to its best end.

I think that God, the universe, or whatever you want to call it, has placed something in us to tell these stories and to move people. It's like the nose on your face, it's there, and it's part of you. There are a lot of people who think actors are absolutely nuts and the last thing they want to do is get on stage and tell somebody a story. Yet, they love us for it. It's a voice that has to come out. Otherwise, the stories aren't going to get told.

WORDS OF ADVICE

- Be brave. Instead of sending out hundreds of resumes hoping that somebody calls you back, target twenty or thirty, and then follow up. You must make those calls.
- When seeking an agent, pick parts that show you off to your best ability in a showcase or play. There's nobody who can do it better than you in that one area, and if you recognize that, it's dynamite.
- Get to really know who you are, how you come across, and what your selling points are. Are you a pink bon-bon, or are you chocolate fudge? If you can accept what you are, then when you approach the agent you both will have a clear idea of where you're going.
- Know yourself as best you can. You have to get your act together emotionally, because it's only from that base that you're going to be able to make the magic.

35

Alfonso Freeman

Alfonso is thirty-eight years old and has been pursuing acting professionally for six years. He is originally from Los Angeles and has trained with acting teachers there. His film credits include featured roles in *Kiss the Girls*, *The American President*, *Seven*, *The Shawshank Redemption*, and a voice-over in *Bopha*. In theatre, his credits include *Man of La Mancha*, *The Visit*, *H.M.S. Pinafore*, *Guys and Dolls*, and *A View from the Bridge*. He has also filmed a commercial for British Petroleum that will be shown in South Africa.

I've always liked attention and I've always been talented in the arts. The thing that kicked me over the edge, though, was watching my dad, Morgan Freeman, succeed. I've always been acting, but I had never gone after it professionally. When I got laid off from my job of thirteen years in aerospace, the next day I said, "I'm an actor." My dad succeeded, why can't I? I decided to challenge myself in the arts because that's where I have my greatest strength, and that's where I have my greatest love.

I'm older now, so I don't have the factor of intimidation that a lot of young actors have. So I'm able to look at things more objectively. In the movie portion of the industry the producers are not impressed with my attachment to stardom. I am a commodity, so I still have to prove myself. My dad has already done that. They are nice to me, but they don't have to give me anything, and they don't. It's not about the name behind you. When you do get there, then of course Hollywood has something to play with, but the fact is, me, the actor did the work to get there, not my name.

A highlight for me is the response I get on stage. It is a gift, and now I am trying to learn how to work it. When I take the bow, I'm basically saying "Thank you" because the audience sat there and watched me perform all night.

The lowest point for me was working with someone who was not a true professional. Professionalism is an attitude, it's not just the training. The actor I speak of didn't exercise control on stage in a fight scene, and I ended up getting physically hurt. As a result, I had to have an operation to repair a broken bone in my wrist. When a scene is choreographed, an actor can't deviate from that because his adrenaline level goes up. *He has to have control!* I'll walk off the set before I'll work with someone like that again. I work very hard to keep this instrument in shape, and I don't need someone to take it away from me by losing control. My body is what I earn a living with as an actor.

Regarding ethnicity, I haven't run into problems so far because I also sing and have been able to do musicals. However, Hollywood can't just do films like *House Party*, where everyone is saying, "Yo, what's up?" They do that kind of film to get the young audience because they make money, but sometimes it can put some quality actors out of work. In real life, most of us aren't like the stereotype. A lot of us come from educated, middle-class backgrounds. The rule is, basically, a black actor has to work twice as hard to get it, and therefore work twice as hard to keep it. That's the bottom line. Of course most of us will do what we have to to get paid, but there is a line that must be drawn for the sake of personal and professional integrity. Each actor regardless of race must know where that line is for him or herself.

When auditioning, I'm learning as I go. I haven't been doing it professionally as long as other actors, but I'm watching, listening, and learning. Just don't panic. You might as well have fun, because there's a lot of other people going out for the same role as you. Even if you know the people you're auditioning for, back off a little bit. Give them your best performance as a professional, not as a best friend.   You could walk away their worst enemy if you don't get the job because you expected them to give you the role because you're their friend. Go in as a professional. Go in knowing that you stand as much of a chance to get the job as to lose the job.

I handle rejection by playing music. I mean, life goes on. I have too many talents to let them all go to waste on account of one. Actors need something that takes them away from the disappointments. If you hit a dry spot as an actor, go see plays and keep your juices flowing. Go to other actors productions and support your fellow artists, because that support will come back around.

It's simply love that keeps me going. It's a romance. I see the big picture. I see everything that's involved with it, not just the immediate day-to-day disappointments. I could walk away from it for those, but I love it too much to let myself get caught up in all that silliness. As a business, this can really suck, but what is it that keeps us going; it's the love.

WORDS OF ADVICE

- Hope is a wonderful thing. Hope is that on which your dreams are based. Keep the hope.
- Take at least ten minutes before you go into an audition, close your eyes, meditate, calm yourself down however you choose, and picture yourself doing the role beforehand.
- One actor said, "Luck is when opportunity meets preparation." When you're prepared you stand a much better chance of getting the job.
- It's more important to pursue an agent from showcasing yourself as a better actor than to go out and get any agent.
- If you don't love it, don't do it!

36

Gayle Rogers

Gayle has been pursuing acting for thirty years. She is originally from Los Angeles, and she received her acting training working on the sets of MGM and Twentieth Century Fox. Her uncle Ed Wynn, and her cousin Keenan Wynn, were both established actors/comedians. As a child she went everywhere with her uncle and observed him. She started dancing at three years old, and before she knew it she was working under contract with Fox and MGM. At age twelve she stopped working, and after graduating college, got a job at MGM as a messenger. From that job, she found herself under contract again. She has made ten films at MGM and over seventy-five television episodes at Universal. She is now performing in comedy/improv and theatre.

I always knew what I wanted to do. There was never a question in my mind. I was exposed to it at a young age, but it didn't mean I had to like it. Sometimes kids can be rejected because they start so young. The only time I was ever happy was when I was working, and I still feel the same way today.

Not only did I work as a messenger on the MGM lot, I also worked for producers in development. I read scripts for them, found properties, and got involved in casting. I could always say I needed to get off at a certain time to audition. So I worked when I worked, and it was flexible. A wonderful thing for actors to do is to get involved in loop groups. Loop groups consist of actors who record background sounds for film and television. With looping you get scale, but you also get residuals. It could be something in addition to your acting income.

My six years at Universal and my eight years at MGM were probably my happiest times because of the amount of activity. The most wonderful thing about my career is to make people laugh. That's a gift. To see someone's eyes brighten in that moment is wonderful because this world can be difficult. When you connect in that way with the human heart and soul, people can put things in perspective so they can laugh. You never stop growing, you never stop learning. I don't think there's ever a point of stopping. Every highlight is a highlight to the end because everything is different and special. My highlight for now, though, is to hear the gift of laughter.

Every time there's a glitch in the road and I'm not completely doing what I want, it tugs at my heart. I think that's why I always keep that in perspective, and never lose track of my heart and my goal. When I'm not doing something I love, nothing quite fits.

I think improv has made a great difference in my auditions. It allows me to make quick decisions and to become automatically focused. I like to go to the audition by myself, and not tell many people. When actors tell too many people they're going on an audition, they set themselves up for expectation, disappointment, and they get more nervous. Whereas, if you go, have fun, and just focus on what you're there for, you won't get blocked. The actors that get called back and get the jobs are the actors who don't go in with baggage. They just go in and let it be. Let yourself be in the moment of what you're doing, as opposed to the expectation. You don't need to be validated by them, and they don't need to be validated by you.

On my first interview I was so nervous I forgot my name. Not only did I forget my name, I read the other actor's lines, and they called me back! They called me back because they thought it was hysterically funny. Thank God it was a comedy. I just had to break the ice of that first interview.

Whatever you're presented with, especially as young actors, never compromise. As a young actress, I went out to read for a casting director and he wanted me to meet another casting director. Everyone was at lunch, but the secretary said there was a casting director in his office who would see me. The office was about the size of a postage stamp. I walked in with my picture and resume, closed the door, turned around, and he was stark naked from the waist down. I gave him my picture and said "Well, it was nice to meet you, please call me if anything comes up." Meanwhile, he was trying to get dressed. I started working at this particular studio a lot, and a year later I ran into him again. This time he wasn't in a little office, he was the head of the department. I was walking with another actor back from the commissary after lunch, and the other actor introduced me to him. He said, "Do you know Gayle?" The casting director said, "Oh yes, but she never comes to visit me." So I said, "Of course I'll come visit you. In fact, I'll visit you tomorrow." I went to his office the next day, and now the office was the size of Dodger Stadium. I walked over to the desk, sat down, and damn if he didn't drop his pants again. So I said, "What is wrong with you? It really makes me feel sad with all these young actors coming in that you feel you have to do that. I'm not saying that I would, and I'm not saying that I wouldn't, but with the way you've asked me, you'll never know." In other words, I politically got out of telling him to screw himself because he could have messed me up by being the head of that casting department. Whatever work I was going to get that way, wasn't going to be work. So, don't compromise, but be smart about it. Never close a door. Always leave a door open because you never know. If someone is a janitor one day, they could be producing a picture the next. Always be the same to everyone.

I was a fighter, so rejection didn't affect me as much. I just kept going to the next thing over and over. If you don't get something, it's not you personally. They may have owed someone a favor, or it could have been pre-cast. It doesn't mean they won't use you for something else. The industry does snowball, though, especially when you're doing film and get into dailies, because other people come and watch.

The business is wonderful in the fact that it is never too late. You can work or start at any age. Life doesn't always deal fair cards, but it's up to you to keep pursuing it. Once it's in your heart, it's the only thing that fits.

WORDS OF ADVICE

- Never give up.
- Never let anyone tell you you should or shouldn't do it. Always listen to your gut feelings.
- Never stop studying and always be prepared.
- Don't have any expectations about stardom, just look to work.
- Remember, no one wants to be the first, but when someone is the first to give you that job, then more and more come after that.
- My uncle Ed Wynn said, "If you have your heart and your mind on what you really want, there may be forks in the road that take you different places, but if you really focus on it, you'll get there."
- I always made a point of thanking directors and casting directors by sending them a note after each project.
- Be open to everything in the business because you never know what you can learn.
- When you go on that set or stage, it's your homework to learn everything about it.
- When you go in for a call-back audition, don't get creative and change it. Actors ruin their call-backs all the time by changing what they did. You are called back because of how you've read. Just come back and do it the way you did the day before.

37

Peter Van Norden

Peter is forty-four, and has been pursuing acting for twenty years. A native New Yorker, Peter studied with Sandy Meisner at the Neighborhood Playhouse. He has a long list of credits on and Off-Broadway. He has acted opposite Kevin Kline in *Hamlet* at the New York Shakespeare Festival, as well as *Jungle of Cities* with Al Pacino at Circle in the Square. His film credits include acting opposite Jody Foster and Kelly McGillis in *The Accused*, as well as *Police Academy 2*, *Naked Gun 2½*, Academy Award–winning short film *Ray's Male Heterosexual Dance Hall*, and as the lead in *Don't Call Me Frankie* at the 1993 Cannes Film Festival. His television credits include a lead role in Stephen King's miniseries *The Stand*, and recurring roles on *L.A. Law* and *Life Goes On*. He also performed a one-man show about the life of Oscar Wilde called *Wilde and Wonderful*.

I was interested in theatre since I was a little kid. My parents were musical comedy buffs, and my father was a major film buff. So I was around it a lot as a kid. While I was still in school I was hired to do a play in Central Park for the Shakespeare Festival. I've been working as an actor ever since. I've never had a job besides acting. The nine-to-five jobs only give you a lunch break in the middle of the day. If you do that, you're going to wake up one morning to find you're thirty-five years old, and you won't be an actor. It's the most common thing in the world. You need to make a living, so you get a job, and all of a sudden ten years go by. If you are going to pursue a career as an actor, you need the freedom, literally at the drop of a hat, to run some place, audition, meet someone, or network.

The film I am most proud of is *The Accused*. I played the defense attorney for the rapists. My fear from reading it was that it would be too issue-oriented. However, the film came out much deeper than that. The scene of the gang rape was enormously disquieting. People asked me why they had to show that scene, why the audience had to see it. I told them without that scene it wouldn't have worked. It's the whole emotional point of the movie. People had to come out of that scene with shock, realizing that whatever she did in that bar, she didn't deserve that.

When auditioning, I try to get off-book as much as I can because I'm just better that way. I can make more direct eye contact with the person I'm reading with, whether it be a casting director, the director, or a reader. I don't have my eyes in the book. There are times when you absolutely cannot do that, you don't have time. In that case, it is better to read it, but still stay in as much contact as you can with the person you're reading with. As long as they can see you have something interesting going on in your reading, they know they can work with you.

In New York I got an agent because he saw my work in the theatre. It's that simple. The agent I got in Los Angeles came from a meeting set up between myself and the head of an agency through a mutual friend. I met with the agent, and I could tell he was not eager to sign me. As I walked out of his office into the hallway, another agent came out of his office, saw me, and said, "I saw you in a film last night. You were terrific." He was referring to the first short film I did, called *Audition*, which played at the L.A. Film Festival. That's the reason they signed me. It was a fluke. So, I don't know how you get an agent. It's the dumbest, most difficult thing to do. Try to get them to see your work. Try to get some film on yourself, perhaps a student film.

There are times when I can really wonder "Why am I putting myself through this?" It's an extraordinarily difficult business. What keeps me going, though, is that when I do work, the experience is, nine times out of ten, a wonderful experience.   Also, I got into acting because I thought I had something to say. This is the way I can express it.   When I find a piece of material that does that, it is a very rewarding experience.   Having the knowledge that I can find something that will really touch people.   Make them laugh, make them cry, and make them think. That is what the job is all about, and that is what keeps me in it.

WORDS OF ADVICE

- If you stick with it long enough, and you're good, eventually someone will notice.
- If you don't have true belief in yourself, then you better get out.   You will be eaten alive otherwise.
- Being able to understand what a playwright is getting at, and how he is trying to get at it, is invaluable to an actor.   You need that technique of knowing how the process is reflected in the actual writing.
- Be able to analyze a script, make decisions about your character based on that script, and then make that come alive emotionally.
- You have to believe that you have something to offer.
- Sandy Meisner used to say, "I'll be an actor, or I'll die."   That's the kind of commitment you will need.

38

Ted Katzoff

Ted is fifty-four and is originally from Washington, D.C. He has pursued acting for fifty years and fencing for forty-two years. As a child, he understudied and performed in the touring company of *Point of No Return* with Henry Fonda. Later, he performed the role again at the Pasadena Playhouse. Ted was a regular on a sitcom called *Professional Father*, starring Barbara Billingsly (before she became mother to "the Beaver" she was mother to him). His television and film credits include *Playhouse 90*, the films *Point of No Return* starring Chuck Connors and Jennifer Jones, and *Storm Center* with Bette Davis. He graduated from Lawrence University in Wisconsin, majoring in theatre, and went on to receive a Masters degree from the University of Connecticut. While at Lawrence University, he started a fencing program that continues today. He taught acting, stage movement, and directing at various schools, which included the UCLA Opera Company. He began teaching fencing as an avocation, which led to opening his own fencing club. He created The Westside Fencing Center in 1984, which merged fencing and theatre. It is a division of the Gascon Institute for Sport Education and the

Arts, which is a nonprofit charitable California corporation. Ted coaches actors for stage, television, and film. He has also worked with Geena Davis and Matthew Modine for *Cutthroat Island*, and Christopher Guest for *The Princess Bride*. He was also fight master on *Outrageous Fortune* with Shelley Long, and *Hook* with Robin Williams and Dustin Hoffman.

When I was four years old, my sister was born and she was not healthy. Since my mother was busy taking care of my sister, she wanted to find a place where I might enjoy myself. So instead of the usual preschool, she found a school that taught drama for children. I stayed with them for five years. Even when I was in regular school, I continued performing with them. I learned my basic acting skills at the age of four. Theatre was something I enjoyed doing. Getting on stage in costume with the lights, having the audience respond, and feeling their presence was pleasurable.

Many years later, I discovered a similar feeling involving a soundstage. When I worked on *Cutthroat Island*, they were doing a screen test with an actor for a lead role and they had rented a corner of a soundstage at Warner Brothers. They asked me if I would help with the fencing. It had been a couple of years since I had been on a soundstage. When I walked in, it was like a jolt hit me. It felt as if a stimulant entered my bloodstream. There is a true emotional impact when you're on a soundstage, even if you're doing practically nothing. I understood then more clearly than ever the call that makes people sacrifice so much to try to be in show business. It made me feel so good to walk in there. It surprised me, actually, because I have acted and coached for years and thought I was used to it. I also realized (because of my own particular attitude) that I couldn't depend upon the entertainment industry for my entire income, and that I was safe. I've seen people give up their whole lives to do, very often, very little. So few are fortunate to be able to do good work on a regular basis.

I worked in retail sales for five years which I hated, but at the time, I had to do it. You have to be completely available because as a choreographer of stage combat, I've been called to do jobs when they said it would only be one day and turned into three days. As an actor, you can't expect that it's going to be what they say it's going to be. It's always going to be longer and more involved. You have to be flexible. If you can't be flexible, you're better off sticking with your job and doing theatre part-time. However, if you're adamant about being an actor, you have to be ready to give up a lot of things. Be ready to leave whatever you are doing to put food on the table, until such time as the acting can be the thing that puts food on the table.

In terms of pure excitement, a highlight was working on *Hook*. Being the lead fight choreographer, I put the team together that did all the training and choreography in the development of the fencing, as well as being a background pirate. Another highlight was at sixteen years old winning the Junior League Championship for Southern California and being undefeated for two years. My students have won national-level championships and have made it to the Olympic fencing team, and that's been very exciting. Also, directing young actors and taking them to a place they may not have been in terms of thinking and emotion has been wonderful.

The low point for me was when I had to work a full-time job. I started out as a mailroom clerk, then was made assistant manager of internal supplies and maintenance. Then the retail company changed hands and I had to work as a clerk in one of their stores, or be out of a job. So I took the clerk position. I took merchandise and moved it from one shelf to another for no apparent reason, and I waited on customers. It was day after day, and I hated it. The work itself was mind-dulling. I became a mule who picked things up and put them down. When I got a part-time job at Busch Gardens as a street theatre performer, I quit the clerk job flat. Then I had to hustle and get a teaching job in theatre by September, which I did.

When preparing for an audition, concentrate on your body movement and voice. In a cold reading, remember to have patience, allow your eyes to see the words on the page, and allow the words to come out of you in as natural a fashion as possible. Don't try to "act" because then it becomes obvious. Let the words begin to create whatever emotions there may happen to be without overdoing it. Learn how to read three or four words ahead on the page so you can flick your eyes up and make eye contact. Most importantly, don't try to be an actor.

Through the production of *Point of No Return* at the Pasadena Playhouse, I got an agent. Agents were in the audience and they called my parents. I was with William Morris, and then a private agency for most of my childhood career in film and television. Los Angeles presents particular difficulties getting an agent; I would say go to New York.

Rejection is the norm. You have to present yourself in an audition as if they're going to fall out of their chairs and take you instantly, but rejection is the norm. That's why I never let it bother me. You have to keep studying, going to auditions, and going to school (even if it's private coaching).

What keeps me going is the fact that acting has been so much a part of my life when I was young that I perform almost naturally. When I am giving talks about what I do, I to a certain extent perform. It's a wonderful feeling, and there's no other feeling like it in the world. You can feel the response, and feel yourself taking words, feelings, gestures, sounds, movements, and turning them into something unique, fun, and different. In terms of stage combat and swordplay, I just love it. I was probably a swordsman for centuries in past lives! I feel very good with a sword in my hand, and I enjoy teaching, because I enjoy communication. That's what acting is as well. So when I teach, I'm communicating and I'm acting.

WORDS OF ADVICE

- Remember that there are ten thousand actors and only ten jobs, but if there's something in you that cannot be fulfilled unless you are an actor, then you take the risk and do it one hundred percent.
- Do equity-waiver or community theatre to keep your skills sharp and honed.
- One important thing about acting, especially in film where scenes are shot piece by piece, is to keep every moment important and worthwhile to you.
- If you're in a dry spell, find something to do. Go to readings, give readings, if worse comes to worst, get a script, get together with friends and read it to each other. Don't lose your craft because you're waiting for someone to call.

39

Richard Kinsey

Richard is originally from Placentia, California, and has been pursuing acting for nearly twenty years. He studied theatre and music at California State University, Fullerton, and has studied voice and acting technique with various teachers in Los Angeles and New York. Most recently in 1996, Richard and his family were in countries such as Singapore, China, Korea, and Africa where he was playing the role of the menacing Inspector Javert in the highly acclaimed International Company of *Les Miserables*. This was Richard's fifth company of *Les Miserables*. The other companies, all North American, were The First National, The Third National, The San Francisco Company, and Broadway. Richard played Inspector Javert in all of these companies and holds the world record for performances of the role. In 1995 he was awarded the Joseph Jefferson Award for Best Supporting Actor and Achievement for his work as Inspector Javert. Some of Richard's other theatre credits include Phantom in the Yestin Koppitt *Phantom*, Quincy Morris in *Dracula, A Musical Nightmare*, Lancelot in *Camelot*, the Pirate King in *Pirates of Penzance*, Jud Frye in *Oklahoma!*, Joe Hardy in *Damn Yankees*, Sky Masterson in *Guys and Dolls*, Billy Bigelow in *Carousel*,

Adam Brant in *Mourning Becomes Electra*, Billy Flynn in
Chicago, and Don Quixote in *Man of La Mancha*. Richard
is also involved with staged readings of new works with
such companies as Playwrights Horizons and The York
Repertory Company in Manhattan. He also composed the
music for *Robin Hood, the Musical*, which won an ASCAP
Award for popular composition. He resides in Los Angeles
with his greatest inspirations, his wife Susan and their baby
daughter Zoe Clair.

My mother was a wonderful coloratura soprano, and they told me that
when I was two years old I started imitating her singing. My mother
thought it was extraordinary, so they started taking me to retirement
homes, standing me on a chair, and I sang to the elderly. That's how I
began, and I performed subsequently in little solo spots, children's
choirs, and rock bands. My temperament has always been artistic and
creative. My freshman year in college, some students told me about
auditions for a theatre company production of *Camelot* and that I
should just try it for laughs. I wasn't going to because I had been
mainly a singer/musician up to then, but I auditioned, competed with an
army of actors, and won the role of Lancelot. I was scared to death.

When I was starting out, I worked as a waiter and bartender. I also
did temp work, telemarketing, convention work, everything having to
do with interaction and communication. Artistically, I sang in churches
as a soloist, performed children's theatre, and was lucky enough to
work at the Birdcage Theatre at Knott's Berry Farm. I did nine shows a
day of melodrama and carny barked at the same time. Carny bark is
when you address the crowd saying: "Ladies and gentlemen, right this
way . . . " Then, I would do dinner theatre at night. Is this crazy or
what? But I loved it.

A highlight for me was performing Inspector Javert in *Les Miserables* for over six years. The experiences that came from doing that
work were extraordinary. It was some of the hardest work I've ever
done in my life. When I did eight shows a week in that kind of a role
that demanded me to be a monster, a powerful creature, and an arche-
type, it took everything I had to make it work. Fortunately, the discipline that I learned beforehand helped me to be focused. Something
wonderful that came out of that experience was meeting some of the
most powerful, famous people in the world and finding out that they
started out as telemarketers also. I also made some phenomenal friends.

I remember one night after I had been on Broadway for six months and been a little stressed out with the pace of the show and all the publicity, I looked up into the rafters of the theatre and thought, "My God, I made it to Broadway. I'm on Broadway." It was an epiphany for me. I went back in my mind to being a little kid singing in a choir, and I realized that all I had done before had prepared me for this moment. It also taught me about endurance because I had to do so much athletically to make the role work. I blew out my knee in the role and had to go on stage with injuries. A commitment to God, the role, and my fellow actors kept me going.

I try to come from all my theatrical experiences in a positive way, no matter what they are. Each experience is teaching us. I hate to be a bore, but I go with that old adage: "There are no small roles, only small actors." After *Les Miserables*, I did a show in Texas called *Dracula, A Musical Nightmare*, came back to New York, and I couldn't find work. There was a show being cast and they told my agent they didn't want to see me because I had done musical theatre, and the show was a musical! They said they didn't want to see anyone who had done a "tra-la-la" type of musical. My agent explained that I had played Inspector Javert, who was not a "tra-la-la" type of character at all, quite the opposite. They still wouldn't see me. I was very put out because they weren't validating me as an actor. I mean, after six years what did they think I was doing up there on stage if I wasn't acting? By the way, one of our greatest villains, Christopher Walken, started out as a song and dance man. I picked up *Backstage* and decided I would show these people that I'm an actor. I saw that they were auditioning the role of Adam Brant in *Mourning Becomes Electra* Off-Broadway. I went in to audition and hadn't done a monologue in four years. I got halfway through the monologue and stopped. I started laughing and told them "I forgot it!" They also started laughing and said, "I don't care. Here just read this." He handed me the script and I read one of the speeches. After I finished, he said "You're hired." So I did the show, got a wonderful review, and I wrote a letter to this person who wouldn't see me for the musical audition. I wrote: "You're right, I can't act, but I'm doing Eugene O'Neill. I guess Eugene O'Neill doesn't need actors, does he?" I never got a response, but I was happy.

After the Eugene O'Neill play, things got tough again for a while and I started to lose a lot of confidence in myself. It wasn't that I lost confidence in my abilities, I'd lost confidence in my career. At one point, a friend I sang with in a church group asked me to sing pieces from *Les Miserables* in concert at the university where he taught. So I sang the role of Javert, and the audience went insane! Keep in mind that I had performed this role in front of thousands of people, I had signed a lot of autographs, but that was months before, and after some hard knocks, I had forgotten about it. When these people started to applaud, I almost looked around to see who they were applauding for. When I exited the stage door, I was mauled to sign autographs. The next week I got a call to do *Phantom*, and two weeks into the run I got a call from Cameron Mackintosh inviting me to come back as Javert. So then I found myself back in the Third National Tour of *Les Miserables*.

The way I prepare for an audition is to vocalize. I try to sing every-day. The foundation of what I sing is Italian, because Italian vowels are the purest, keep the voice the healthiest, and always keep me ready to do what I need to do. I'll even do that if I have an audition that doesn't require me to sing, simply because acting for me is very physical. I need to have it in my body. I feel that if I vocalize and breathe I'm ready to do certain things. I also pray. I pray a lot. It centers and fo-cuses me, and I feel that God is behind what I do anyhow. I also go in with the attitude that I am the best for the role. I don't go in thinking "they're not going to like me." I embrace an audition. I don't like them any more than anyone else does, but I look on them as a challenge. Challenges are glorious and keep us sharp and poised.

I remember performing at the Carmel Bach Festival while I was in final auditions for *Les Miserables* and they were getting close to making their decision. They kept telling me "We can't tell you anything, but don't take any other roles." One night I was out running. It was very dark, and as I came over a hill, the moon was very bright and it illumi-nated a lagoon. I can't explain it, but I knew the minute I saw the light coming down on that lagoon that I had the role. The next morning they called me, and I had the role.

If you're seeking an agent you need to have a real sense of who you are. It's imperative. You have to start back at the basics. If you go in with pretension or trying to sell something that you're not, that's really going to smell. We do create illusions, that is our profession, but act-ing, to me, is painfully honest. If you're not exhibiting that honesty in your daily life, how are you going to exhibit it on a stage or in front of a camera? A camera doesn't lie, and an audience knows when you're lying. You have to take care of yourself and be comfortable to be able to exhibit authority. The idea of the "starving actor" living in a slum, and living on Cheez Whiz is not my idea of being comfortable. Get your personal life together, get well grounded, and move on from that point. Then get the best pictures you can, because your picture is your calling card. They might cost more, but get the best pictures you can. Also, *do not* pad your resume! Put together any good reviews you received as well, because that's something you can submit to an agency. If you're being showcased in a play, send postcards out to agents. I really feel that agents and casting directors are *for* us. They want the best product they can get. After all, they have to sell it!

I'm better with rejection than I used to be because auditions aren't that precious to me anymore. We can't take it personally, though, because we may see ourselves one way and somebody else may see us another way. It's kind of like being in a police line-up. They call it "typing." I'm O.K. with it now because of the success I've already had. I also feel if it's God's will that I do something, I will do it, and if it isn't, I won't.

What keeps me going is that I love what I do. It's what I was born to do, and I feel it's what I'm best at. Nothing in life is guaranteed, no job is secure. With corporate downsizing, they can't give you a lecture any more about how acting is the most insecure job in the world. It's not realistic. It's inspirational to do what I love. It's in the marrow of my bones, and that's why I do it. I also have wonderful support from my wife, daughter, family, and friends. Their support has been a *key* factor in my perseverance and success.

WORDS OF ADVICE

- Don't think you're too good for a role, because you're not, and you're going to learn from it.
- Artistically, if you think "Well, I've arrived! I'm going to sit back now," you're finished! Pablo Picasso went to the Metropolitan Museum of Art when children's art was being exhibited. He walked in and said weepingly, "I know nothing. I have to start over," and he was seventy years old at the time.
- Keep filling your cup, and know everything you can know about acting.
- Know your spiritual values and self-worth. Make these the foundation of your life.
- Live your life to the fullest. Art is experiential, and that is what we communicate to the world.
- Love your family and friends with your whole heart and let them do likewise with you. Listen to their words and let them support you. We are only alone if we choose to be.

- Yes, you are crazy to be an actor, but so is the rest of the world, so you're in great company.
- Don't forget to laugh!

40

William Schallert

Mr. Schallert is seventy-five and originally from Los Angeles. He has pursued acting for fifty years. Since he began acting professionally in 1947, he has done more than 50 stage plays, 80 theatrical films, 650 television episodes, numerous radio shows, and several thousand voice-over commercials. Recently he co-starred as Judge Omar Gaffney in the Hallmark production of *Harvey* for CBS, and he is probably best known for starring as the father on *The Patty Duke Show*. He also sired *Nancy Drew*, all the *Little Women*, *The New Gidget*, and Wendy Malik on *Dream On*. From 1991 to 1992 he starred as Boarder Hodges on NBC's *The Torkelsons*. You can also find him on *Nick at Nite* as Dobie Gillis's teacher, and as the ancient admiral on *Get Smart*. In 1980 he received an Emmy nomination for daytime drama for *The Stableboy's Christmas*. In 1995 he starred with Jane Kean in *On Golden Pond* in Denver, then played Gaston in the Steppenwolf production of Steve Martin's *Picasso at the Lapin Agile* at the Westwood Playhouse. He also starred as Dr. Pangloss/Storyteller/Martin in Leonard Bernstein's *Candide* at the Ahmanson Theatre. Previously, his stage work brought him a 1971 Obie Award for his performance as The Judge in Daniel Berrigan's *The Trial of the Catonsville Nine*, and has twice been honored by the Los Angeles Drama Critics. Among his theatrical films are John Huston's *The Red Badge of Courage*, *Lonely Are the Brave*, *In the Heat of the Night*, *Colossus*, *Charley Varrick*, *Teachers*, *Innerspace*, and the *MANT* section of Joe Dante's *Matinee*. He was also the voice of Milton the Toaster for Pop Tarts for many years, and the voice for Green Giant, Polaroid, and countless others. He was president of the Screen Actors Guild, a Governor of the Motion Picture Academy, a trustee of the Motion Picture and Television Fund since 1975, and of the SAG P&H Plan since 1983; and on the Board of the Permanent Charities Committee of the Motion Picture Industry. Mr. Schallert received the Ralph Morgan Award from SAG in 1993 for service to the union.

I didn't set out to be an actor, but when I was in school and we had to read aloud in class, I was aware that the other people were not making much sense out of it. I'd think, "Boy I wish they'd call on me, I know I could do better." I could always make the words on the page sound like it was just me talking. I could make it my own. In high school I won a couple of public speaking contests, but I didn't associate that with being an actor. To me, actors were leading men, like Clark Gable or Tyrone Power, and I didn't look anything like that, and I wasn't interested in being a second banana.

Then, when I was at UCLA, a director named Blossom Akst cast me in *Volpone* as Corbaccio, a lecherous eighty-five year old miser. I didn't know how to really act yet, but I had an instinct for playing outrageous characters, and that experience got me hooked on acting.

After the war, I did some more acting at UCLA, and then joined a new theatre group in Hollywood called The Circle Players. I did about 25 plays with them the next four years and, gradually, I got started doing small parts in movies, radio, and then television.

I had never really studied acting at that point, I just learned on the job. Along the way, I did join a couple of workshops, and about twenty years later I even studied with Sandy Meisner and afterwards, with Bobby Lewis. I know it would have helped to do that when I was starting, but still, you have to have the basic talent. Acting is like sprinting: good coaching helps, but nobody can teach you how to run fast.

It was slow going, though, in the early years. Strother Martin started at the Circle too, and we were both starving the first six or seven years, but neither of us ever did anything else besides acting. Other actors I knew would get a job somewhere, and if it paid well enough they'd get used to the money coming in and pretty soon they'd stop acting. You should only get temporary jobs that you really hate if you want to act. Acting is a freelance occupation and if you can't tolerate the uncertainty, it's probably not for you.

Once, for about four months, I did try to sell water softeners in my spare time, but I lacked the ability to "close," so I never even sold one. Eventually, someone stole the demonstration kit out of my car and I lost the deposit. That convinced me I was doomed to be an actor. Fortunately, my wife was an actress, so she understood and never pressured me. I never would have made it if she hadn't believed in me.

In 1952 I got a Fulbright Fellowship to study the British Repertory Theatre system and for almost a year I had to stop acting. The first film I did after we got back, I was not good in. There's an object lesson in that for young actors: it's crucial, especially in the early years, to keep working at the craft of acting as much as you can. Whether it's in a class, in a play in a little grungy theatre, or in a workshop. If you don't work, you lose the sense of yourself as an actor. You've got to act. I remember getting (if I was lucky) $10 a weekend for two performances in a small theatre, but if the show worked and I felt good about the performance that night, I was a killer the next week at auditions. I'd get almost anything I went out for because my sense of myself as an actor had been confirmed by the audience. It's crucial for young actors to do that.

About auditions: obviously, first you should read the script. The problem in Hollywood is that producers only want to give you "the sides"—two or three short scenes taken out of context that you are actually going to audition with, even though they are supposed to have a full script available. I was president of SAG in 1980 when we got that provision in the contract, but the casting offices will tell you they don't have a full script. I always say, "where did you get the sides? It says here page 52, page 53, that came from a script somewhere." You have to insist on the script, because you can't evaluate a role without it. You won't know if it's worth doing unless you see the whole thing. More to the point, you need the information in the script to understand the context of your part. It's just crazy that they're so reluctant to let you see it. If there's time, I always try to learn an audition scene, because it frees me up to connect with the other person and really act. But, if there's not time to learn it cold, you have to just read the scene. You can't do it half one way and half the other.

Which brings up the question of stage fright and nerves. We all suffer from them to some extent, especially on opening nights and at auditions. We know we're being judged. There's only one cure for it: get involved in what you're doing. It's the moment before you start where the nerves happen and Sandy Meisner gave some very good advice about that moment. He said, "Preparation is very difficult to talk about. In the long run, before you go on stage, you do your preparation. If it doesn't work, if you're not in the right emotional state, when your cue comes you still have to go on stage. So, go on, and start doing what the character is supposed to be doing and, in the process, you'll get involved in the scene whether you've prepared properly or not." That applies to auditions too, in my experience.

About getting an agent: if you look like Cindy Crawford or, maybe, Arnold Schwarzenegger, that'll probably do it. However, for most of us, the best bet is to work on stage. You can't generally begin on Broadway and you can't generally begin in a major movie. You're most likely going to begin by working in a small theatre, maybe with other actors who are starting the theatre. Work in a small theatre, and pretty soon your work will be seen (if the theatre is doing good work). People will begin to come, the word will get out, and the first thing you know a casting director or agent will talk to you. There's no simple way to do it, but you have to start somewhere. Just keep going and eventually someone will decide you are the person they want. That's how you get the first jobs, by working in a venue where they can see your work.

The reason I've kept acting for the last fifty years is that I needed the money—and I'm not kidding. Becoming a "star" is not something you can really work at. The public makes stars and they either take to you in that way, or they don't. Once I realized it was out of my hands, I decided that acting was just my job, the way I made a living, and I got on with my life. I didn't know where else I could make a living and get as much satisfaction (certainly not selling water softeners!). I love working with an audience, especially making them laugh. I love living the imaginary life that you live when you act, creating the character and his life in such a way that they seem totally real to me and therefore, to the audience, but I also love getting paid for it.

Early on in my so-called career, I decided that the most important thing to me was my family. I feel fortunate that besides acting on stage and on camera, I also had success in voice-over commercials. It enabled us to live well, and I didn't have to travel to locations all over the world to stay employed as an actor. I could stay here in Los Angeles, be at home with my wife while my kids were growing up, and have a normal life. Not all actors are that lucky.

WORDS OF ADVICE

- Shop around for a good teacher. Ask other actors about their teachers, or find out where another actor studied.
- I would recommend going to Los Angeles, New York, or Chicago for the best teachers and the best place to start out.
- There's an advantage for actors who want to work in Hollywood to establish themselves in New York first. If you come out from New York with a reputation and a smart agent, he can set a moon high price for you. You will be a new commodity. Hollywood is a funny town because many times actors get pigeonholed early on.
- Be sure you keep acting in whatever venue is available to you. Keep moving from one theatre to the other until you find a place that suits you.
- It's very important to be professional about your work. Be disciplined, be on time, and solve problems, don't create them.
- You have to be flexible once you're doing the work. For one thing, the set may be nothing like you imagined, especially on location. There are also a lot of distractions on any set while you are shooting. The director may have a totally different approach than what you've figured out at home while you were learning the part. In spite of that, you still have to function professionally, keep your cool and do the work.
- You have to be able to respond to what's in your imagination in a truthful fashion. Meisner said, "Acting is behaving in imaginary circumstances truthfully. Not interestingly, not amusingly, not dramatically, but truthfully." The basic acting talent is the ability to behave in the imaginary circumstances as if they were real, but it's the choices you make, the ways you behave under those circumstances that define your talent as an actor.

Selected Bibliography

INSPIRATION AND MOTIVATION

Angelone, Gina M. (Producer), James Lipton, (Executive Producer), Joshua White, (Producer/Director). In the Moment Productions. *Inside the Actor's Studio*. Television series. The Film and Arts, Bravo Network.

Byrne, Gabriel. *Pictures in My Head*. Niwot, CO: Roberts Rinehart, 1995.

Caine, Michael. *Acting in Film: An Actor's Take on Movie Making*. Revised edition. New York: Applause, 1997.

Canfield, Jack, and Mark Victor Hansen. *Chicken Soup for the Soul*. Deerfield Beach, FL: Health Communications, Inc., 1993.

Cohen, Robert. *Acting Power*. Palo Alto, CA: Mayfield, 1978.

Grodin, Charles. *It Would Be So Nice If You Weren't Here . . . My Journey Through Show Business*. New York: Random House, 1990.

UNBLOCKING CREATIVITY

Cameron, Julia. *The Artist's Way*. New York: G. P. Putnam's Sons, 1992.

——. *The Vein of Gold*. New York: Tarcher-Putnam, 1996.

Maisel, Eric. *Fearless Creating*. New York: Tarcher-Putnam, 1995.

Taylor, Terry Lynn. *Creating with the Angels*. Tiburon, CA: H. J. Kramer, 1993.

MARKETING AND AGENTS

Callan, K. *The New York Agent Book*. Fourth edition. Studio City, CA: Sweden Press, 1995.

———. *How To Sell Yourself as an Actor*. Third edition. Studio City, CA: Sweden Press, 1996.

———. *The Los Angeles Agent Book*. Fifth edition. Studio City, CA: Sweden Press, 1997.

Charles, Jill, and Tom Bloom. *The Actor's Picture/Resume Book*. Dorset, VT: Theatre Directories, 1991.

Cohen, Robert. *Acting Professionally*. Second edition. Palo Alto, CA: Mayfield, 1975.

Henry, Mari Lyn, and Lynne Rogers. *How To Be a Working Actor*. Third edition. New York: Watson-Guptill, 1994.

Hines, Terrance, and Suzanne Vaughan. *An Actor Succeeds*. Hollywood, CA: Samuel French, 1990.

Katz, Judith, and Katinka Matson. *The Working Actor*. Revised edition. New York: Penguin Books, 1993.

O'Neil, Brian. *Acting as a Business: Strategies for Success*. Portsmouth, NH: Heinemann, 1993.

———. *Actors Take Action: A Career Guide for the Competitive Actor*. Portsmouth, NH: Heinemann, 1996.

AUDITIONS

Bens, Paul G., Jr., and Ellie Kanner. *Next: An Actor's Guide to Auditioning*. Los Angeles: Lone Eagle, 1997.

Hooks, Ed. *The Audition Book*. New York: Watson-Guptill, 1996.

Hunt, Gordon. *How to Audition*. Revised edition. New York: HarperCollins, 1995.

Oliver, Donald. *How to Audition for the Musical Theatre*. Revised edition. Lyme, NH: Smith and Kraus, 1995.

Shurtleff, Michael. *Audition: Everything an Actor Needs to Know to Get the Part*. New York: Walker and Company, 1978.

JOBS

Alterman, Glenn. *The Job Book, 100 Acting Jobs for Actors*. Lyme, NH: Smith and Kraus, 1995.

———. *The Job Book II: 100 Day Jobs for Actors*. Lyme, NH: Smith and Kraus, 1995.

Jacobson, Deborah. *Survival Jobs*. Los Angeles: Windtree Publishing, 1996.

Index

About the Author

STARRA ANDREWS is an actress and writer. She earned a B.A. in Theatre at the University of California, Irvine and completed Los Angeles City College Theatre Academy's Acting program. She currently lives in Los Angeles.

ISBN 0-275-95692-X

HARDCOVER BAR CODE